How to Build the Gambia
Attaining Economic Super-power Status in Africa

Yaya Sillah

Suba Kunda Publishing

http://www.subakunda.com

subakunda@yahoo.com

+2209459540

ISBN-13: 978-9983-953-68-8

INTRODUCTION

In the name of Allah, the most gracious, and the most Merciful, praise be to Allah, lord of all world. May Allah shower his blessing on our prophet Muhammad (PBUH).

The Republic of the Gambia used to be part of the Manding Empire. The first recorded history of the Gambia appeared in the late 17th century, from an oral tradition, narrated by musicians, Islamic scholars, Christian missionaries and the like. It was around the 12th century AD that the first humans from different parts of the Manding Empire began to gradually occupy lands in sub-Saharan Africa, including the Gambia. However, it's not clear who the first settlers were and which tribes they belonged to, or what the origin of the name Gambia is, and why they gave such a name to the country. However there are a number of theories about the meaning of the name, the origin of the people who live in the country, what language they spoke, their culture, religion and so on. It's almost impossible to verify these stories because of the oral tradition: in the early days, nothing was written down. Those who narrated the history may have just done it for entertainment purposes or to follow their own personal agenda.

The National Museum and the National Centre for Arts and Culture provides valuable information for those who are interested to learn the history of the Gambia. The Republic of the Gambia has much natural beauty and wild life; and the country is well known for its rich culture as well as the courtesy and humility of her peoples. This tiny smiling coast of Africa was also affected by transatlantic slavery and European colonisation.

The information contained in this book mainly comes from my own opinion and personal political experience, but includes some sources from Gambian newspapers.

I am taking the opportunity of our newly found freedom of expression to express my opinion and my understanding of the history of the Gambia. Just few months back, before the 2nd of

December 2016, to publish a book such as this in the Gambia was equivalent to kissing a woman on the lips in a busy market in Riyadh. You can use your own imagination as to what I mean by that. The objective of the book is largely centred on the political atmosphere since Gambia gained independence from British colonial rule, and especially the political impasses which erupted after the December 2016 presidential election.

Most of the information and stories in this book are short excerpts from the wider political spectrum. I summarise the major political and social events which took place in the Gambia; particularly from 1994 to 2017. This includes the rise and the fall of President Jammeh as well as the political and economic challenges facing the Gambia in the post-Jammeh era.

I also discuss why Gambians decided to let the Jammeh government rule them for more than 22 years and why Gambia has decided to vote him out, which forced him to relinquish power and go into exile.

I must point out that I am neither a politician nor an economist; however I have great interest in both subjects. In the past few years, I have conducted political and economic research in the Gambia and I have contributed immensely to socio-economic development. As I stated in my previous book Marriage and Society, it's a moral obligation for every citizen to participate physically and intellectually in his or her country's national development efforts; hopefully this book will aid that purpose.

CONTENTS

CHAPTER 1
MY PREDICTION OF MILITARY GOVERNMENT

In the early 1990s, the Gambian economy was booming under the PPP regime and freedom of speech was every citizen's right. However, the public were increasingly impatient and yearning for regime change. President Jawara, who occupied the highest office in the land for nearly thirty years, was ageing and the rumour of corruption at high levels of his government ignited the Gambian citizens' eagerness for a new dawn. Imminent change of government was an everyday topic for Gambians.

I remember one evening in September 1993 in particular. While drinking green tea Hataya with my family friends, including Kemo Jaiteh, in my uncle's compound at Serrekunda Bundung, I predicted that one day there would be a military government in the Gambia. I'm not sure how I knew that. Maybe my enthusiasm for military uniforms was the start of my political instinct. In my early days, I could only dream of reading newspapers and I obviously had very little political experience. But because of my interest in politics, I made sure I closely followed with keen interest almost every major political event in the country.

The main sources of information for me in those days were the radio, and physical interaction with politicians. I made sure I listened to Radio Gambia news as often as I could. Such curiosity in politics was very prevalent in Gambian youths.

Sometime in mid-1994, shortly before the military coup, I was lucky to be among the crowd at Serrekunda Ebo Town when the then vice-president of the Jawara regime, Alh Shieku Sabally, with his wife and entourage, visited Ebo Town Mosque. He held a very constructive meeting at there with the Ebo Town community and the PPP party militants in the area. I can still vividly remember he looked very smart in his traditional waranboo Gambian dress and eye glasses. At that gathering, Sabally promised the communities in the area development in the form of road projects, a market for women vendors, and to renovate their main mosque. I think that particular meeting was one of his last official public functions before the military took over the government.

One day around that time in 1994, I was in Standard Chartered Bank opposite the Police headquarters in Banjul, assisting my Uncle Alahassana Cessay with some financial transactions. To our surprise, the police set up road blocks in the area due to the pending inauguration of the new police headquarters by the then President of the Gambia Alh Sir Dawda Kairba Jawara. As a curious young man wearing long dress whites embracing the summer heat of the Gambia, I patiently stood and waited for the arrival of his Excellency. A few moments later, President Jawara appeared in his presidential motorcade with a convoy of his cabinet ministers and other government officials. He was wearing a black business suit and necktie, wearing his trademark eye glasses. That ceremony was one of the most beautiful political ceremonies I ever witnessed. After observing the usual presidential protocols, the official opening of the new police headquarters began with music played by the Gambia Police Band. President Jawara delivered a short speech, after which he returned to the State House. A short while later, we left Banjul and returned to Serrekunda. If I remember rightly, that occasion was also one of President Jawara's last public engagements in the country before he was pushed from power by Lieutenant Yaya Jammeh and his supporters.

Before the military coup in 1994, life was nothing other than normal in the Gambia; no-one suspected the Gambian army was preparing to unleash a dramatic sequence of events until Thursday July 21st, when it was announced in the evening news of Radio Gambia that the US Military were present in the country and they would conduct joint military exercises with the Gambian army. Strangely enough it was the same day President Jawara returned to the Gambia from London. The following day, I was woken by a phone call from my uncle

Alh Mbemba Suwareh from New Jeshwang, who asked me to drive him to visit some family and friends around Serrekunda. I met him and his party at Jeshwang at around 10a.m. A few minutes into our journey on the main road near the Alh Sankung Sillah factory junction, we saw a group of women who intended to go to Serrekunda market for their daily food shopping, running back towards our car. I decided to stop and I asked them what was going on. To our surprise we were told there was a military demonstration taking place, relating to their late salary payment. I quickly turned around and told my uncle "It's not true". I'd heard on the radio the previous evening about the planned joint military exercises and I assumed that was what was taking place. I decided to proceed with our journey.

Our first stop was the compound of our local MP, Mr. Mamadou Saydyone: we soon noticed his great frustration and confusion. The situation was very tense. My uncle asked him what was happening in the country; he was not sure what was going on, neither could he managed to reach anyone by phone. While we sat in his living room, he noticed his telephone line had suddenly stopped working. We left his place around 11 a.m. and continued our journey to Serrekunda London Corner, to see Alh Morro Gikineh. Once there, he advised us to return home immediately as sources within in the government had told him there was a military coup taking place in the Gambia. After hearing that shocking news, I felt the mood in the house dramatically change and I could see panic in people's faces. Without delay we jumped in our car and rushed back to Jeshwang. Could you believe it? My car ran out of fuel at Serrekunda Grand Mosque. I went look for petrol around the market, but all the petrol stations in the area were closed. I managed to organise a taxi for my uncle to Jeshwang and I continued with my struggle to find petrol; by 1 p.m. Serrekunda was in total chaos. The news of the military coup spread like wildfire. At Westfield junction, an off-duty military officer, roughly dressed in half a uniform, approached and warned us that civil war could erupt. While at Westfield, I saw military officers confiscate both private cars and taxis. I returned home without my car feeling very miserable. At 3 p.m. Serrekunda was like a ghost town.

However, I managed to persuade some of my close friends to accompany me to Serrekunda Mosque junction and they helped me push my car all the way to Ebo Town. As we approached Churches town, we met a large truck full of military men stationed at Babung Fatty junction; they instructed us to leave immediately and they added that if we wanted to know what was happening, we should go home and listen to the radio. At this stage everything was calm: no violence or public harassment. We did as instructed.

The declaration of the second republic

As Friday came to an end and it looked as if it was going to rain at any minute, I can only describe the mood of Serrekunda as sombre. The atmosphere could only be compared to a month of Ramadan. Can you imagine fasting for a whole month without water and food? As you approach the evening with intense thirst and hunger, you are counting every minute as it goes by. That was exactly how it felt in the Gambia. Our source of information was limited to one commercial radio station. The other two stations, Radio Gambia and Radio Syd, were closed for business (do you know; in the first republic there were only three radio stations in the Gambia; one owned by the government and two commercial?).

I remember we were all gathered in one place like cattle at the river bank staring at the radio with intense eagerness waiting for the news. It felt like football spectators who were waiting for their team to equalise. Amazingly at 5 p.m. on Friday 22nd July 1994, the voice of a well-spoken soldier was heard on Radio 1 FM and he announced in English that the country was under military rule. Before he could even finish reading the statement we jumped up and started to celebrate the new dawn. Guess what? We were not alone; it prompted weeks of jubilation in the whole country. I think our celebration was genuine because at that time, most Gambians were yearning for change; it was not out of ignorance and envy of the former PPP regime, as some people suggested. A few moments later, the voice of the same soldier was heard again. This second time, I made sure to listen to his full statement. I remember he said the constitution was suspended, land and sea borders were closed, and there was to be a temporary curfew from 7 p.m. to 7 a.m. until further notice.

According to the statement some cabinet ministers had been detained and those who had not were to report to the nearest police station. Later in the same evening we learnt that President Jawara, along with his family and some cabinet ministers were unharmed and they had fled to neighbouring Senegal. As usual there was much speculation as to why the military overthrew the Jawara government. What mesmerised most Gambians is how it was possible to overthrow a government which had served the people for thirty years without a single gunshot, or drop of blood spilled.

It was just matter of time before conspiracy theories engulfed the nation. At first President Jawara was accused for secretly planning the military coup so that he could enjoy an early retirement! Some peoples suggested that the CIA, in collaboration with the Nigerian army, helped the Gambian army push Jawara out of the way. Gambians were left in the dark as to who was their new leader and why the democratically elected government had been overthrown.

The new rulers of Gambia

On Saturday 23rd July 1994, Gambians were informed of their new leader and his intentions for the country; that morning's announcement from Radio Gambia woke up every Gambian from their bed. According to the state media, an armed forces provisional ruling council led by Lieutenant Yaya Jammeh was the new government of the state.

Later that afternoon, they revealed the full list of the military junta: "Lieutenant Yaya Jammeh is the chairman of this new ruling council, Lieutenant Sanna Sabally is the vice chairman, Lieutenant Sadibou Hydara is the spokesman and Minister of

5

the Interior, Lieutenant Edward Singhateh is Minister of Defence and Lieutenant Yankuba Touray is Minster of Local Government and Lands."

The new cabinet included four civilian men and women. However, all the district commissioners were military officers. Gambia soon got used to life under the military. Regular checkpoints were installed at every major strategic point in the greater Banjul area. Radio Gambia soon became the platform for frequent announcements of military decrees which replaced the constitution. Public demonstrations were strictly forbidden.

Gambians would have to wait for few more days before they could set their eye on their new leader, however. On Monday 25th July a picture of new Gambian leader appeared on the front page of the Daily Observer. I can still vividly remember how innocent-looking young chairman Jammeh was. In that picture, he wears a military camouflage uniform with a red military beret on his head; in his usual mood of confidence - mouth closed, pointed face, no smile, gentle and serious.

Within hours of publication; self-appointed historians were quick to unveil his biography; but after a while when the dust settled we realised many historians had got it wrong. It's wasn't the Yaya Jammeh who used to play in the army football team, neither was it the Yaya Jammeh from the Tamba Jammeh Iliasa family. He was Yaya Jammeh, nicknamed "Kanilai", not well known publicly, but well known within the Gambian army, and people from President Jawara's inner circle were no stranger to him. According to those who knew him before 22nd July, he was an officer from the former Gambian national gendarmerie, a single man, a serious soldier, with an ambition to become great one day. Guess what? That was proved to be 100% correct.

It didn't take long before Jammeh and his council mates became the darlings of Gambian youth. And I was no exception: for me it was just matter of time before I found myself in the middle of a Jammeh fan club, even bearing the nick name of "Chairman".

Chairman Jammeh wasted no time in telling Gambia and the world why he led the military to overthrow the Jawara regime. Jammeh and the ruling council who later became his disciples conducted a series of public meetings and media briefings to earn the trust of Gambians and get much-needed public support. He travelled the length and breadth of the nation to sell his vision of transparency and accountability to a sceptical public. There were many different accounts as to why the PPP regime was toppled. However, Jammeh in his speeches and the official statements of the AFPRC stated that there was rampant corruption in the PPP regime, there was nepotism, President Jawara had stayed too long in power, and there was a lack of infrastructure development as well as lack of job opportunities for youths.

The military junta easily convinced the whole nation and international community to rally behind them; and they cleverly used the momentum which they gathered from the start to their advantage. Apart from the British government's travel advice to their citizens to avoid all non-essential travel to the Gambia, the following two years of transition was nothing other than a honeymoon for the junta.

During the two year transitional period

For the next two years there was no really significant international pressure on the AFPRC government. However, they faced unrest at home. From November 1994 until the general election of September 1996, multiple failed coup attempts were said to take place. The most shocking of all was the alleged coup masterminded by Lieutenant Basiru Barrow and, later, another alleged coup by Jammeh's own friend and vice chairman, Captain Sanna Sabally. Despite all that, Jammeh and his council members managed to survive and led a very comfortable life. Some of them got married, including Jammeh himself to Madam Tuti Faal. He later performed the hajji as a pilgrim to the holy city of Mecca. In 1996, while the general elections loomed, for chairman Jammeh and his council members, it was time to accumulate titles. Jammeh was promoted through the ranks and decorated from Lieutenant to Alh, Captain, Lieutenant Colonel, Professor and so on and so forth. For the next 22 years, more titles were added.

Meanwhile; Gambians carried on with life as normal in the land of "milk and honey". As usual with no quarrels, the Smiling Coast of Africa carried on smiling; and waited like a babysitter while hoping the military junta would deliver their promises. The 22nd July Movement, headed by Mr. Baba Kajally Jobe, was working to plant Jammeh in Gambian hearts, minds, bodies and souls. The unforgettable slogan of the day was "Power to the people - transparency and accountability". Mr. Jobe and other Jammeh disciples prophesied that it would only be Yaya Jammeh who could lead the Republic of the Gambia to a prosperous future. They persuaded Gambian elders to convince Yaya to resign from the Gambian army and contest the coming general elections. Gambian generosity gave Yaya Jammeh many rewards including land, cows, sheep and goats. Gambian people named their chidden after him and his wife. There was no shortage of publicity in the country; some went to great lengths to compare his personality and leadership qualities to that of prophets like Yahya, Moses, Solomon and Muhammad.

Consequently at the end Jammeh was invisible. In the early stages of his reign, when he spoke in the public, his accent sounded Nigerian and his physical appearance resembled former Burkina Faso Renaissance leader Thomas Sankara. Gradually he started to imitate Cuban president Fidel Castro while his political philosophy was exactly that of Libyan leader Muammar Gaddafi. He adopted many traits of Gaddafi including his green flak jacket; and the former Nigerian leader Sani Abacha was definitely an influence on chairman Jammeh. Can you imagine mingling and socialising with those unpredictable guys that some were already labelling as dictators, some as lunatic, and some as authoritarian? Jammeh was hoping to emulate them.

The 1996 food shortage

In early 1996, Gambia faced frequent essential food shortages, especially of rice, flour and cooking oil. One morning I remember we ran out of rice and I couldn't find even one cup in any of our local shops. I was told there was government rice for sale at Churches town fire station. On my arrival I nearly had a heart attack when I saw about a kilometre long line; hundreds of people queued to buy rice. I stood like a police officer for almost six hours before I could manage to lay my hand on a bag of rice which was on sale for D160.

This became a frequent occurrence in the Gambia for at least a few months. Chairman Jammeh blamed the business community for it and accused them of sabotage. It was very obvious Jammeh would not compromise with anyone to increase his chance of winning the incoming election. Jammeh used all his executive power to divert the resources of the Gambian government and engaged in business of all kinds. With the influence and help of a few enablers he quickly attracted and hijacked the clients of major business in the country.

On the other hand, the business community in the Gambia blamed the government's rapid increase of duty and sales tax on lack of foreign aid and inflation. Did you know that in the 90s, twenty percent of Gambia's GDP was totally dependent on the tourist sector and tourism industries? No tourism meant lost revenue; at that stage, the country's economy was at all-time low. However, for Jammeh, almighty God was his new IMF and World Bank; in his own words "whether it's financial assistance or economic growth, God will always come to rescue Jammeh".

He never hid his contempt of Western super powers for "looting Africa's resources" and their role in transatlantic slavery and European colonization of Africa; to add the salt to the wound they were now "sabotaging his country's economy by banning travel and freezing aid". The cat and mouse game between Jammeh and the European Union would continue to the end of his tenure.

The 1996 general election

Before the 1996 general election; the AFPRC created the IEC (Independent Electoral Commission) which would observe all elections in the Gambia. Political parties in the Gambia were jockeying to join the race for the State House. Some former members of the ousted PPP, and the NCP with their sympathisers, struggled to find a suitable candidate to challenge chairman Jammeh, who had already been convinced by so-called civil society and country elders to stand for election. However, they finally managed to hand-pick the experienced lawyer Ousainou Darboe as their candidate for the newly established United Democratic Party (UDP). The Gambian people were very excited and eagerly waited for the election.

By now some names needed to change. Let's take out the letter "F" from AFPRC and pretend that nothing happened; instead of the Armed Forces Provisional Ruling Council, it was now the Alliance for Patriotic Re-orientation and Construction, or APRC. The unquestionable leader for this new brand would be that of the former chairman of the military junta who resigned from army in order to contest the general election as a civilian candidate: even he also added letters to his name. Instead of Yaya, it was now Yahya AJJ Jammeh. Was it out of desperation or was it a mythical dream of an invisible holy man?

By now most senior officers in the Gambian army were relegated to become Jammeh disciples; only few of them managed to retire and carry on with their normal lives. In any transition there are always casualties; the one time Minister of Finances and Economic Affairs Mr. Kourru Cessay mysteriously died in his ministerial vehicle in unknown circumstances. According to government report his demise was due to fire which engulfed his Mercedes Benz. Many citizens did not buy that story: the media and the people pointed their finger at the military government.

Another case involved one-time council member Lieutenant-Captain Sadibou Hydara: after been sent to prison for an alleged plot to overthrow the Jammeh regime he died in prison; with no clue as to what happened to him. The former spokesperson of the military junta Captain Ebou Jallow was said to have absconded with millions of government dollars, a claim he constantly denied. According his own words from an interview he had with the Freedom newspaper, those accusations were "false and baseless and fabricated to tarnish his image." He promised he would "clear his name at any legal institution in the Gambia" if it was required for him to do so.

The end of transition was the beginning of an exodus for many Gambians to the wilderness of the opposition benches; some went in self-imposed exile to United States, Europe and neighbouring countries; others spent time in the notorious Mile 2 prison and other detention centres. The commission of inquiry established by the AFPRC regime confiscated assets and properties from former PPP ministers, permanent secretaries, managing directors, and their accomplices. The military government did not spare any they suspected, especially those who used to be very close to Jawara and the PPP regime. "Corruption is not going to be tolerated at all costs", Jammeh stated in one of his speeches.

The flamboyant lifestyle which was introduced by the former PPP regime and halted by the military regime would soon be allowed once more. Kanilai would soon become the second capital city. It hosted many traditional wrestling and music festivals, and Jammeh's centre for Experimental African medicines and his farms, where he introduced the slogan of "grow what you eat; and eat what you grow". Gambia was then the home for the International Roots Festival. It attracted thousands of black African Americans and Europeans with a curiosity of Africa and its culture (did you know that Alex Haley's famous black African American

11

character Kunta Kinteh, from the book Roots, originally came from the Gambia?). During the transitional period, the honourable Louis Farrakhan also visited the Gambia. One positive aspect of the AFPRC's foreign policy was to promote African, and in particular Gambian, culture around the world. This reinforced the idea of black people around the world seeing Gambia as their second home.

Under the AFPRC regime, many development efforts took place. Hundreds of primary, secondary, and high schools were built around the country; and for the first time in Gambian history a television station was opened: Gambia TV, which later became GRTS. A number of hospitals including the AFPRC general hospital in the Farafenni North Bank region were built and the existing health centres and clinics were renovated and upgraded to improve their capacity. Roads and bridges were constructed in the greater Banjul area, Brikama western regions and North Bank region respectively. Communications and infrastructure developments are the key component of economic growth; to create a better society with millions of job opportunities is a mere fantasy if it isn't supported by adequate medical facilities and schools. Why are there so are many conflicts and senseless wars around the world? Those are all the fruits of the ignorant. Lack of education means lack of self-awareness, lack of employment, lack of health, and lack of anything essential.. but I digress.

When the election campaign started, four registered political parties - namely APRC, UDP, PDOIS and NRP - were scrambling for supporters like children assembled under the mango tree, patiently waiting to grab the falling mango fruits. The intense political atmosphere surely would not show any mercy to the short, smart-looking, male lawyer Ousainou Darboe, whose profession was to steal the suspicious hearts and minds of judges in the court room. With all that weight of support and wealth of intellectual experience, for him, facing the nation loaded with millions of promises by the newly appointed ruler felt like a primary school boy giving a lecturer to sceptical professors at Cambridge University.

Darboe would have to wait for many years before he could dream to walk through the door of the State House.

The day after the elections, when every vote was counted, Jammeh comfortably won the election with an impressive majority. He now became His Excellency Retired Colonel, Professor Alahaji Yahya James Junkon Jammeh, President of the second republic of the Gambia. Meanwhile; the former childhood sweetheart of the chairman, first lady Madam Tuti Faal Jammeh, had long disappeared to the wilderness: the new darling sitting in the throne at Statehouse Banjul was an African/Arabian beauty queen with a round face and long neck called Madam Zainab Zuma Jammeh. She comfortably exercised all her rights and would not shy in displaying her beauty to any women who thought they might replace her. Gradually they all vanished into thin air; never to be seen again. For the next twenty years she would never compete with anyone for the title of First Lady of the Gambia.

Now; let's close Chapter One by determining why the sequence of events described in this chapter occurred, but before we do, I would like to bring the following statement to your attention: I never served in any capacity in President Jammeh's government. Neither does it intentionally harbour any grudge against me. I think it's worth me pointing out that I never personally meet President Jammeh or any of his close associates during and after the transitional period, or indeed his entire 22 year rule. However, from the beginning of his tenure in office, I was obsessed with his government and fascinated with Gambian politics in general.

During the first seven years of his leadership while in the Gambia, I followed him with great interest like a bee follows honey. I attended many of his political rallies.

I can also say the same about President Jawara, but I was born during President Jawara's reign and when he was removed from power I was still a young man; as a result in regards to his biography, I relied heavily on second-hand information, as well as passages from his own book *Kairaba* which I read like a romantic text message. Additionally, I am "neutral for now": I don't belong to any political party in the Gambia. My opinion is not politically motivated; neither do I have a grudge towards anyone. I was very impressed when I heard President Barrow use my slogan "One Gambia, One People" in his inauguration speech on 19th January 2017 in Dakar, Senegal.

Let's play political pundits together. Did you know that the Republic of the Gambia was the victim of transatlantic slavery and European colonization? Gambia had been in such a state for many centuries: some say for four hundred years. However in the middle of the 1950s, calls for independence and self-rule increased dramatically. White British colonial masters were under a lot of pressure to comply with that demand. In those days, only a few institutions offered education to children from the ruling elite's family and minorities who served as clerks for colonial masters. A handful of those who were privileged to have access to education in the country began to create local political parties to challenge the colonial masters and achieve independence. As we now know, the People's Progressive Party (PPP) was one such political party.

We should note that all English speaking countries in West Africa gained their Independence through peaceful means, without conflict with British colonial masters.

Dawda Kairaba Jawara, Gambian-born but later educated in the United Kingdom, was an ordinary veterinary officer who became the leader of the PPP and was in charge at the time of independence. Jawara is a very interesting character: it was his good fortune to attain independence, much like a shopkeeper winning a lottery jackpot. and in totally different circumstances from the likes of Nelson Mandela. According to reliable sources, Kairaba Jawara was neither politically active nor a revolutionary fighting to gain independence by force; he was merely approached by the PPP who requested him to lead the party as well as for him to stand as their candidate for the coming election. This was not without

14

controversy: a reluctant Jawara would have to consult his father first before he could reach to any form of agreement with the PPP. With his father's approval and blessing; Jawara led the PPP, and the country, to independence on18th February 1965.

You might ask yourself the following question: how is it possible for a veterinarian who profession is looking after animals to be amazingly successful in leading humans out of the misery and persecution which they had endured for many years? Here is my answer: all that it takes for men to achieve great things is life is intellect, understanding, humility and confidence. Jawara had all of those attributes. He has a great personality. He is proof of the saying "if man has mercy for animals, he has mercy for mankind" (note also that in 1950s America the black civil right activist Martin Luther King was in a similar situation when he was approached by black community leaders who requested him to lead their civil rights movement).

Finally, it was time to abandon old-fashioned colonial governorship and install Jawara as Prime Minister for the newly independent Gambia. It was a daunting task, like flying to Mars in a small aeroplane, to rebuild the country from scratch. Jawara was prime minister at first: it took many years before the country became a republic and Jawara became president: for thirty years, Jawara and the PPP faced many difficulties in rebuilding Gambia and her institutions.

In July 1981, a group of rebels lead by Kukoi Samba Saniyag attempted for three days to overthrow his government but they failed, thanks to timely military intervention by neighbouring Senegal forces. Hundreds of lives were lost and millions of dollars' worth of properties were lost, damage and destroyed. As far as I know, there were not many threats to his personal life except in the 1980s when the helicopter he was travelling in had an accident in which one of his friends died.

Note that rebellion is prevalent in third world countries

especially after gaining independence from colonial masters. There are number of factors which may cause this: foreign interest in their natural resources, foreign intervention in internal politics, proxy wars sponsored by a foreign power, religious conflict, tribalism and government corruption.

Did you know that Jawara is well decorated with many medals and honours including the knighthood from Her Majesty Queen Elizabeth II? (in the United Kingdom it's a committee chaired by the office of the Prime Minister which recommends people to the Queen for knighthood; the selections are usually drawn from the list of people who contributed immensely to national and international development, as well foreign dignitaries and leaders from the Commonwealth).

He has performed the Hajji, the Muslim pilgrimage to the holy city of Mecca (Hajji is an annual religious events which is held in the holy city of Mecca once every year. It includes rituals and constant reflection in reminding the faithful of the importance of devotions to worship Allah. It's compulsory on every Muslims to perform Hajji at least once in their life time. It's the fifth pillar of Islam).

President Alahaji Sir Dawda Kairaba Jawara and his government have created almost 75% of all Gambia's institutions; and they were credited with many developments initiatives, including health facilities, education institutions; freedom of speech, freedom of expression, freedom of liberty, multiple party democracy, human rights and good governance. President Jawara played a crucial role in promoting international peace and he is among the famous world leaders who advocate for peace, freedom and liberty. He stood in solidarity with the people of South Africa and Palestine in their respective fights against apartheid and Israeli occupation.

You might wonder, with that impressive track record, why anyone would want to remove Jawara from power.

Towards the end of his political career, you could understand that he may have been emotionally exhausted; thus Jawara surrounded himself with long-time party loyalists, the majority of whom later became like family members. However, there was constant public rumour of high level endemic corruption existing in his government. Members of his cabinet capitalised on his generosity: it was unimaginable for him to sack any corrupt officials or expel any member from his government.

At some point when he realised this, in the early 1990s he wanted to step down from office but his friends acted like Mile 2 prison guards: they wouldn't let him go. Meanwhile the Gambian army were boiling with anger at being long removed from the driving seat and reduced to a ceremonial role. For the army, regime change was an everyday topic; and taking the country by force was an option.

Power struggles compromised the PPP: government ministers positioned themselves to fill the gaps; it would soon become apparent that something was going to happen. It was a race against time between the apostles of Vice President Alh Shieku Sabally and the military wing guiding his Excellency; a violent change of government was imminent, and it was entirely dependent on who was the luckiest and whose disciples would fire the first shot.

Innocent citizens would soon be caught in the middle of a raging fire. Other political parties in the country were long out of equation. Come 22nd July 1994, President Jawara would be forced to run to Senegal with the two most important women in his life, Lady Claine Njaie and Njemeh Mbouge. Ten years passed before homesickness kicked in; after his return to Gambia in 2004, he had to get used to normal life without the trappings of office.

Key point of interest: Gambia is a country where people still believe in the divine right of kings. This means whoever comes to power is there by the will of God; and therefore they should be given 100% respect: opposing them means opposing the will of God. Thus to change the nation by democratic means is almost impossible. Interestingly such a concept   used to be the position of the western society around the world; however, in the late 15th century, a British political philosopher, Thomas Hobbes, was credited by his fellow European philosophers as suggesting that social contract is more fitting than the concept of the divine right of kings. Eventually, this intellectual view became the belief system of the political class.

Social contract is the basis of today's political agenda, but before Africa was exposed to globalization, the ruling elite were allowed to stay on the throne for life. The next king would rise to the throne to replace the former king. Occasionally trouble might erupt if the successor failed to live up to the expectations of the people.

Competition for power and influence could mean waging war against an opponent; but desire for this kind of conflict to gain political leadership in Africa was a rare occurrence before contact with European people. I am not suggesting there was no ethnic conflict among different tribes; of course that existed, but usually such conflict would involve farmers fighting to control land and external aggression with intention to invade indigenous lands.

The arrival of Christian missionaries and contemporary Islamic scholars who were wholeheartedly welcomed and accommodated by indigenous African rulers who share common interest with them by ensuring that due respect is always available to their counterparts. Political leaders and their subjects equally share social responsibility in that.

Despite the increase in globalisation these customs still exist. Even today, those who exercise power, and people who fill the important political positions in towns and cities across Africa would follow such traditions. Alikalo in small towns, mayors for large cities, sub-Alikalo for small villages, district commissioners, and leaders in compounds are usually selected from the ruling elites. The philosophy behind this concept is the divine right of kings. It's extremely difficult for someone to acquire a leadership position if they don't belong to the family lines of people in power.

In the case of Presidents Jawara, Jammeh and Barrow; if you ask the reason why they ascended to the throne, you might argue they were destined for it. This is what I call the second avenue to climb the ladder of leadership: it's a miracle for those men to become President.

Some claim that their fate was predicted by unknown holy men who prophesied their coronation long before they were even born; sometimes, it is luck for those men to be born in a land where myth and superstition control the status quo. No one questions your competence or qualifications. While self-appointed sheiks and invisible holy men act as God's agent on earth with duty to guard the divine right of kings, the phenomenon will remain widespread across the world.

Six Gulf countries - Saudi Arabia, Kuwait, Oman, Qatar, Bahrain and the United Arab Emirates - are all ruled by family dynasties; son succeeds father or brother succeeds brother. There is very little chance for others to ascend to the throne. Additionally the second avenue to the ladder of leadership is reduced due to the rapid increase of religious conservative movements in the region. There is little room for common sense in a society where people adhere to uncompromising religious beliefs with strict interpretations and uphold traditional roles. In such an environment you might argue a dictatorship is more likely than a Western style democracy. African politics is quite different from the Western method; in the West peoples usually join a political party based on their social positions - right wing, left wing etc - as well as a love of the party's economic policies. The political atmosphere in African countries is usually based on tribes, regions, and shared belief. Right wing and left wing politics is still a distant dream. Though most people in Africa consider themselves as religious conservatives, this usually doesn't translate into politics.

For example in the Gambia during the first republic there were four main political parties - PPP, NCP, GPP and

PDOIS. Their party members and supporters were largely tribal based. This still continues today. In the case of Gambia, Mandinka, Fula, Sarahul, Jola, Wolof and other ethnic minorities are all equally contributing to national development. However, the country's economy, socially and politically, is largely distributed among the Mandinka, Fula and Wolof communities, while the Sarahul community usually engages in commercial and business industries. The Jola and other ethnic minorities dominate the manual labour force and security. This may have triggered the feeling of being marginalised by some members of Jola communities in the country. As a result Kukoi Samba Saniyag attempted to overthrow the PPP regime in 1981 and President Jammeh subsequently succeeded in July 1994. This theory is my opinion; anyone who reads this book has the opportunity to come forward with their own version of events.

The final segment to this forensic examination

The removal of Jawara from power is strikingly similar to the removal of former Ethiopian emperor Haile Selassie I. Selassie reigned from 2nd April 1930 to 12th September 1974, during which time his government made many tremendous social and economic developments in the country, particularly his quest for Africa to unite by creating the Organisation of Africa Union (OAU). He personally took centre stage in helping several African countries to achieve independence. Peace prevails in Africa thanks to his foreign policy.

In relation to Ethiopian sovereignty, there is no doubt one can safely argue that without his talent as leader, Ethiopia would have plunged into civil war and there would have been no security in the country, exacerbated by the climate of frequent fear of foreign invaders, particularly Italy. However, despite all that, in the mid-1970s, Ethiopians felt economically and socially neglected by his government.

Civil disobedience became frequent, triggering the military to take power from him. Unfortunately for Haile Selassie, he and his family were subject to extra-judiciary powers and it is widely believed that he was assassinated by the Ethiopian army. In contrast, President Jawara and his family had managed to escape harm to take asylum abroad. He briefly stayed in Dakar, Senegal, and later went to the United Kingdom, where he remained for at least ten more years; until in late 2004 when he finally received amnesty from President Jammeh's government, which allowed him to return to the Gambia as a private citizen. He remains one today.

According to Ibn Khaldun, a 13th century Arabian sociologist and political philosopher, in his book *Muqaddimah*, when a ruling dynasty reaches the twenty five year mark, usually they no longer represent the public interest. Their desire to stay in power and their hunger to accumulate wealth inevitably generates corruption and subsequently the resources of state would divert to the ruling elite. When such behaviour became prevalent in society, citizens would feel marginalised, perhaps even disfranchised, which would trigger something Ibn Khaldun called "group feeling", which encourages civil disobedience; in the worst case scenario, it would create popular uprisings against the ruling elites as we frequently see in Africa and the Middle East.

The key component to stop this from happening is limiting presidential terms of office to two five year term limits. Public officials should serve those who they represent and create equal opportunity for all, maintain transparency and accountability with good governance, and make the democratic process open and accessible to every citizen.

By now; I think, you have a clue as to why the Gambian army staged the military coup on the 22nd July 1994. However, I will bring one last idea to your attention. If you remember back in the early 1990s, after the civil war erupted by different warring factions against President Samuel Doe's regime in neighbouring Liberia, Gambian soldiers were among the ECOMIG troops sent to Monrovia to keep the peace in the country.

Can you imagine: already disfranchised military youths with

ammunition in their hands were now exposed to war. This would ignite the feeling of men who were already contemplating unleashing this experience back home. It's just matter of time before regime change in Gambia became a reality. You can also say that the Gambian army at this stage were desperate for attention from the Gambian public. They wanted to do whatever they could just to show the nation they were capable; and used government corruption as an excuse to hide their agenda. Hence the Gambian public perceived the PPP government as public enemy number one.

A widely held belief is that, on 22nd July, senior military officers in the army who were loyal to vice president Alh Shieku Sabally planned to stage the coup and overthrow the government. However, Lieutenant Jammeh and his team quelled that and rose against the State House to challenge Jawara.

Is it because of this reason that Alh Shieku Sabally was not given amnesty by the Jammeh government which would allow him to return back to Gambia? Time will tell.

Another question: why was lower-ranking Lieutenant Jammeh chosen to lead the nation after the successful coup?

There are conflicting reports as to why Jammeh was made chairman. According to some military sources, before the coup was staged, there was no pre-recorded agreement among them as to who would fill the government posts. The situation was like school children planning to steal the headmaster's wallet; if it's successful, let's equally share the contents and if it's not, the youngest boy will take the blame for it.

If we say he took the post on merit, well, Jammeh had attained the rank of Lieutenant long before many of his friends and maybe based on this, he was eventually nominated to be the chairman by senior officers within the army. At this juncture they appointed him to the position of chairman of the AFPRC and leader of the country. I am hoping Jammeh will eventually release his biography, and we can finally learn what he says about this.

It's tempting also to ask the following question: why in the following years did the army allegedly try so hard, and so many times, to overthrow Jammeh's government?

Like a husband who caught his wife in the bedroom kissing his best friend, was it from envy and jealousy, or did they soon realise they had made a terrible mistake in choosing Jammeh to lead the country?

CHAPTER 2
MY VISION TO IMPROVE EDUCATION IN AFRICA, PARTICULARLY IN THE GAMBIA

My vision for English and Western education

Just a little over a century ago, English schools were established in African colonies. These school and colleges have given support to the civil services and the wider community. Many thousands of local students in our sub-region, especially in the areas of governance, record keeping, agriculture, science, maths, information technology and more, were educated at these establishments. In addition, hundreds of thousands of people received their academic qualifications from these educational institutions; many graduated with high quality education, ethical and high moral values, discipline and other social skills. However, the conventional way of obtaining knowledge is gradually shifting online. This increases competition globally, especially among the rich nations to control information technology in the modern world. On the other hand, it has created challenges to people living in the developing world, who find it difficult to get access to this expensive equipment. As a result, educational institutions in third world countries are facing many different challenges. These include poor training facilities in school grounds, large numbers of teachers do not receive adequate training to teach in their chosen fields, the general building structures of many schools are outdated and most schools are not equipped with modern day teaching equipment to facilitate suitable education for children.

As a result, many students leave school with basic qualifications from these educational institutions. Consequently, a number of young people are ill-equipped to enter the world of work. In some extreme cases, some young people even lack self-discipline and good manners which makes it almost impossible for any social mobility. An increasing number of students currently studying in Western educational institutions in our sub-region are not motivated to pursue any further education, job training or tertiary education. We think some of these underlying issues have contributed to the large number of youths taking the often perilous journey to Europe. However those who made it to Europe with little work experience or insufficient academic qualification, usually end up being exploited in the labour market or earning their living through criminal means such as dealing drugs and theft.

In order to find a solution which could help to create an ideal environment to ensure a quality education for every child, job skills for youths, and better employment opportunities for young people in general, I would like to make certain recommendations to relevant authorities. Although there are no easy solutions to these challenges, I still strongly believe my recommendations may serve as a guide which could provide solutions to the growing number of challenges in this field.

My recommendation for Governments

1: Education must be the first priority for any government which must ensure that sufficient funds are allocated to the Ministry of Education which will be enough to sustain the Ministry to undertake their development efforts accordingly.

2: The government should ensure that the structure of school buildings is regularly inspected to guarantee the safety of school children. In addition all the school buildings must be equipped with modern essential equipment to facilitate the dissemination of information and knowledge to every student.

3: Governments should ensure there are enough schools with research centres located in every region, with enough teachers and adequate teaching materials are available.

4: The government should provide adequate reassurances concerning remuneration for teaching staff with suitable transport systems where necessary.

5: The government should ensure there is a suitable

mandatory teacher training scheme in various fields.

6: The government should introduce strict regulations to make sure parents send their children to school. In addition, they must prevent parents negatively interfering in their child's education.

7: The government should ensure that outside scholarships are only allocated to children from disadvantaged family backgrounds as well as to children with learning difficulties. They should create job opportunities to school graduates as well as offer skills training to those with less academic qualifications.

My recommendation for teachers

1: Teachers should ensure that they subscribe to all government teaching codes of conduct and respect the roles of designated school authorities in addition to checking their backgrounds in cases of any criminal records or if its required by relevant authorities whenever its necessary.

2: Ministry of education in collaboration with teachers or with teachers unions should ensure there is a cordial working relationship between themselves.

3: Teachers should ensure they follow all the guide lines and school dress codes at all times. They must realise that teachers are not only providing information to children but they are also seen as role models to children.

4: Teachers should ensure school classrooms are not accommodated beyond capacity. They should also ensure respect for teachers in the classroom is always maintained and reasonable discipline for those who might neglect that.

5: Teachers should have a scheme which will notice and support the most intelligent student and those with special talents to ensure they get all the necessary support. And they should ensure children with special needs and those who are not performing well are not neglected. They should equally get all kinds of assistance whenever it is necessary, even if it means additional class room teaching assistant.

6: Teachers should encourage every student not to only rely on computers for writing but hand writing as much as possible. While the students at the same time are also encouraged to read books as often as possible and inspire each other in writing and reading. The information in relation to indigenous scholars should be made widely available which will surely inspire children to do more research both at home and schools. The ministry of education should empower the teachers to introduce in the curriculum the finding of local researchers, experts, authors, and societies.

7: Ministry of education should gradually update the national curriculum in line with modern day require knowledge. They must also use the local resources to obtain knowledge rather than the resources of international experts, where necessary.

My recommendation for students

1: Curiosity is the key for striving to broaden your horizons. This natural gift shell always remains true in the back of every child mind. Parents should ensure this is always the case. Parents must make sure children receive home training as well as how to behaviour in school and society in general.

2: Concentration and paying attentions to lectures in every subject is essential to enhancing understanding which will strengthen your ability to achieve your endeavours.

3: Student should spend a significant amount of their time reading books and writing manuscripts, including doing all homework, research, studies, and physical exercise. They must reduce the time spent in computer games, watching television, hanging out with friends and utilise every free time for doing something useful. Maintaining discipline and good manners is essential in every aspect of human life. It will generally help children to become better adults in the future.

4: Every student should ensure they choose to study the subject of their own accord whatever field that might be as well as not allowing their parents or teachers to impose it on them. It is worth remembering that, in life, people achieve meaningful lives because they are passionate about what they do, which increases the desire to succeed. It is important to introduce religious and moral values in children, as well as teaching them social skills such as relationship, marriage and general ethics from an elementary stage. Also learning different languages and job skills will eventually help to earn a living.

5: Every student should have good role models, mentors, and competitors. While having admiration for role models, it is important that students strive to discover their strengths and weaknesses.

6: Students should be open-minded to new experiences; they must always prefer to find the solution in logic and rational thinking, rather than mysticism and superstition. It's always helpful to be critical and be curious in your thinking, and to do your own research.

7: School children should always be encouraged to display their talents, share their experience, and express themselves whenever it is necessary to do so. They should not feel shy to share their own theories about the world and its inhabitants.

My recommendation for parents

Parents should see their children as blessings, not assets. In order to be a better parent you have to invest in your children's wellbeing especially in the area of health, education, and protection, to the best of your ability. Apart from health, there is nothing more important in a child's life than education; you must ensure it is the first priority for you and your family. You must engage in your child's education at every stage and at any cost.

It is my desire to help to address some of these issues which I have highlighted. However, with very limited resources, I am unable to do so at this stage. Although my Foundation is in its infancy, I have already received so many requests for assistance; I am therefore very hopeful that I will eventually be able to play a more active role in educating the youth of Gambia.

My aim is to promote high quality education for every child whilst helping children to learn work skills.

My vision for Islamic education

For many centuries, traditional learning centres such as Majilis have provided Islamic and religious education to many thousands of local students in our sub-region. Hundreds of thousands of people received their Islamic education from those educational institutions with high quality education, morals, ethical values, discipline and many social skills. However, with globalization and the diversity of many traditions and cultures in the modern world, we have noticed a number of challenges facing these learning institutions. These include a declining number of parents showing an interest in this educational structure, a lack of proper training for teachers, children lacking self-discipline and good manners. As result the increasing number of student currently studying in Majilis are not motivated to pursue any further training or tertiary education. Following my research to find a solution to some of the challenges facing Majilis in our sub-region, I would like to make recommendations. The Government should ensure they provide adequate support to Majilis across the country, equal to that which they provide to English education institutions.

My recommendation for teachers

1. All the learning centres must consider providing at least a two year teacher training course to all their teachers.

2. Teachers must not compromise the core values of Islamic principles such as good character, and improve their physical image, for example, their dress code and general etiquette.

3. Teachers must be selected by merit, not due to their family background.

4. Teachers should introduce the writing and alphabet in a local language, a model of which must be followed by every

student.

5. Teachers should introduce maths, geography, history, at least one foreign language and physical education into the Majilis education system.

6. Every topic must be allocated to a certain group of students and there must be a target of when it should be completed.

7. A strict timetable must be set for every aspect of study.

My recommendations for students

1. All male students must be required to wear traditional long African attire (Haftan) with a hat.

2. Every student must be encouraged to sit on the floor mat, crossing their legs and paying attention to the teacher.

3. Students must be selected to learn in groups according to their level of understanding.

4. Each day, every student must maintain silence during the whole period of learning, without any interruption.

5. Majilis students should be encouraged to practise writing, and reading aloud.

6. Every student must be given the opportunity and encourage to study in other fields outside of Islamic discipline, e.g. western philosophy.

7. Majilis Students must be encouraged to interact socially with other students from different learning centres across the country, particularly English and Arabic students.

My recommendations for academic and intellectual development for the sub region

I am campaigning tirelessly through my charity by using the radio, print media, online social media and individual advertising agencies, in order to encourage local scholars to start collecting and preserving ancient African manuscripts and poetry, which can be used for research and experiments.

In addition, we are persuading academic scholars and intellectuals at all levels to increase writing in the areas of recording keeping, story books, agriculture, African cultures, traditional African medicines, religious rituals, poetry, geography, history, maths, and much more. By the year 2050, 60% of academic materials which are needed for local learning centres and schools could be got from these local resources. I would like to see more improvement in people's desire for increasing research and inventing resourceful materials from their own ideas.

Social and religious gatherings

There are many annual events taking place across many countries in our sub-region such as annual Ziyarahs, Gamos, conferences, weddings, and naming ceremonies. However, with usually loud noises from the ground and the lack of a central topic, this has usually reduced the benefit often expected from these gatherings. We believe it could be more beneficial and useful if certain guidelines are followed. This can involve organizers and speakers at each event focusing on the real life issues facing individuals and society.

My recommendations for social and religious gatherings

1. Each event could be based on a structure and format by selecting a master or chairperson for each event.

2. In the case of events such as Ziyarahs, Gamos, wedding ceremonies, naming ceremonies where the organizers usually choose to recite the holy Quran for seeking blessing and mercy from Allah, they must emphasise to everyone that the holy Quran must be recited with all due respect, as it is stated in the holy Quran itself. That is: be clean yourself, and the actual place of recital should also clean. Pay full attention to the recital, without distractions from people passing by, using mobile handsets, people sitting next to you, television screens, computer laptops, tablets, radio: indeed avoid all electronic devices during the whole period while the holy Quran is being

recited in that particular event.

3. Each of those annual events must be focused on a particular subject matter (theme) which will be the centre of all topics. Additionally, all distinguished and invited guest speakers should be notified of their assigned areas beforehand.

4. When it comes to giving speeches at any major Islamic events in this sub-region, it usually starts with elders or senior scholars first speaking. However, I will recommend the following; at any major events after the introduction of distinguished ladies and gentlemen by the event master or the chairperson of that event, the first topic should be presented by junior and young scholars according to their merits and experience, followed by the top speakers. I think this is much more diplomatic and more honourable for elders and senior scholars. It could also protect and strengthen the position of our religious scholars and traditional leaders just to prevent those honourable men of society from making small errors and certain mistakes.

Finally, the guidelines which are stated in this book are not intended to cause offence to anyone or target any particular Majilis or learning centre. It is my vision for intellectual development in the sub-region. In conclusion, as I stated before; if I have enough resources in the future, I am willing to offer help to any learning centre on the points which I have highlighted. I desire to give intellectual support to anyone at any time.

The challenges facing Madarashe education in the Gambia are similar to those faced by other educational institutions across the country; however with one major exception. Lack of employment opportunity is more prevalent among Madarashe school graduates than their counterparts. The reason for that is usually the Madarashe field of study is mainly focused on the issues related to Islamic laws, Islamic ethics, worship and rituals. Hence the more attractive field of employment for them is usually in Islamic teaching and leading Muslims in congregations in mosques. Usually professions like farming, spiritual healing, manual labour and local business workshops are not desirable to them, in contrast to Majilis students.

Madarashe as well as Majilis students in Asia and Africa are the target of recruitment for Muslims with extreme views. They are targeted on the internet and at community gathering places. However, the traditional methods still remain active. This includes offering free scholarship to students mainly from the Middle East and North Africa. Prospective students who manage to travel to attend those international education institutions are often exposed to radical views of Islam as well as getting access to hateful intellectual material in the form of books, manuscripts and contact with dangerous individuals who eventually would introduce the following to them: hate and intolerance of other religious beliefs, lack of tolerance to modern civilisation, violent behaviour towards political opponents and persecution of religious minorities.

This recent world-wide phenomenon is a challenge to all nations. Sub-Saharan Africa was largely immune to this threat until the late 1990s when it suddenly appeared in Algeria, Mauritania, Morocco, Mali, Nigeria and Niger. Those countries are now all victims of radical Islam; it's just matter of time before other countries experience a similar plague. Usually the brains behind this radicalism are link to terrorist groups originating from the Middle East and adherents of scholars who received their training in Arabia. This is indeed is a cause of concern for everyone.

Madarashe and Majilis students should be made aware of the dangers of radical views and hateful material.

My recommendations for government

1: the government of the Gambia must ensure they introduce strict roles which will monitor every scholarship intended for Gambian students, particularly those studying Arabic and Islamic education. This will serve as a deterrent for recruiting agents. In addition there must be a control mechanism which would ensure the host countries and their educational institutions provide scholarships for educational purposes only. You might ask yourself how this will work. I will explain.

The Gambian government should start to collect data on terrorism and engage in intelligent sharing with other countries around the globe. This data sharing will help the government to determine how many individuals who graduated from those countries and their educational institutions have committed terrorist offenses or engaged in terrorist activities. They can use this information as evidence to withdraw existing scholarships and put those with a terrorist tendency under surveillance.

2: the Gambian government should create a two year training scheme for scholars who complete their studies and intend to disseminate information by using public platforms such as preaching on radio, TV, and in the mosque, as well as using the positions of Imam. Such training will enhance the awareness of individual scholars in respect of the country's culture, and traditions, as well as the government rules and regulations regarding anti-social behaviour. This measure would equally reduce any pre-conceived negative ideas they might hold against the communities.

3: the Gambia government should create equal job and business opportunities for those who graduated from Madarashe and Majilis schools. This will enable the citizens to lift themselves from poverty, which is the cause of most crime. In addition Madarashe and Majilis schools students must be encouraged to broaden their horizons and study other disciplines such as agriculture and medical science.

My recommendation for parents

Parents must ensure they are always there for their children and offer whatever support they can to their children, especially during the period of their education. If parents notice any radical behaviour in their children they should not hesitate to inform the relevant authorities.

CHAPTER 3
HOW TO EARN PEOPLE'S TRUST AND CONFIDENCE TO VOTE FOR YOU

Politics is the art of the possible. But sometimes it's the art of the smart game. Every society has their own way of dealing with peoples. Perhaps the campaign rhetoric which elected someone in Europe would not get you elected in America. However, there are some general issues which might affect all humans in every society: security, the rising cost of living, healthcare, education and so on. But the negative or positive impact of these is different for every society. Let's first examine some international success stories before we talk about the Gambia.

In 1997, the former British Prime Minister Tony Blair used the rhetoric "education, education, education" which was greatly credited for his landslide victory. In that election period, the UK was facing many different economic challenges but education was the main talk of the town. Blair took the opportunity to capitalise on that, and eventually won the election. At that stage; education was not the top social challenge facing British society but it was a major concern of the people. My take on this: as a politician it's really important to seize the opportunity of the topic of the day to use as a tool to earn you popular support, even if it's irrelevant to you. If people are talking about it, make it your first priority.

In 2008 former United States President Barack Obama impressively won the US election using the simple rhetoric of "Yes we can". My take on this is that when society is negative towards a race or tribe or a behaviour, in order to steal hearts and mind, you must give them a massive reassurance like Obama did with that simple sentence. The subtext was "Yes, we can elect a black man as president". And guess what? It worked for Obama. On that occasion Obama didn't tell them "Yes I can". Obama tapped in to American consciousness to make them understand that it was their collective responsibility for the first time in history to elect a black man as US president. Equally his political rhetoric made people feel guilty if they didn't elect him has president. "Yes we can" reinforced the hope of those who always believed "Yes we can". And equally it strengthened the morale of those who believed all along "No we can't." The smart rhetoric brought two sides together as one powerful force to say "Yes we did."

The next story is crazier than the other two above. It stunned the world in 2016. Some people still refuse to accept the fact that it's a living reality that Donald Trump is in the White House. When the US business tycoon declared his ambition to run for the White House, it was the joke of the century. No political pundit ever predicted such fantasy will one day become a reality; but Trump, armed with his massive business skill to win the big contracts would use that skill to steal voters' hearts; in the end it was easy for him to steal America from the grasp of Hilary Clinton. Trump's rhetoric of "Let's make America great again" earned him the keys to White House. If you ask yourself why the already great America would give a chance to Trump to make America great again.. well, the logic behind Trump's victory is simple. He threw doubt in people's minds that they are less valuable and worthless and he had the solution to fix that. However he didn't give any details as to how he would make them great again; in that rhetoric details didn't matter. What mattered here was headlines. This political tactic worked perfectly for Donald Trump.

As a politician in the Gambia, what lessons could one learn from these successful stories?

If you carefully analyse the cases of Tony Blair, Barack Obama and Donald Trump, in the political rhetoric which delivered success for them, they have all used headlines, not details. We might say they have done their homework beforehand and found the social factors behind the scenes to determine which issues are more relevant to voters. Not necessarily what is good for them, but what is relevant to them and they capitalised on that which delivered the result for them. However, there are slight differences in the way each of them pursued the voters.

In Tony Blair's case he used his rhetoric as a wakeup call. In Barack Obama's case he used the rhetoric to build people's confidence in order for them to realise "Yes they can." In Donald Trump's case he used the game of reverse psychology to make people feel that they are not great and he will make them great. In each of these cases, the gamble worked.

But for politicians it's important to bear in mind that generally, political slogans and party rhetoric from the past may not work in future elections. Because during each election campaign, issues which concern the electorate before may not be the same issues as those that concern them now. But as human beings it's almost guaranteed for any politicians to understand that there will always be relevant social issues which matter the most to electorates. People will expect you to give them assurances which are different from the past. For modern politicians, psychological preparation is very important and they always bear in mind that the next election will be different to the last. It's therefore essential for politicians to keep doing their homework. Knowing the social factors beforehand strengthens your ability to set an effective agenda for an election.

I would like to use the situation in the Gambia as example. The country has seven different administrative areas: Banjul, KMC, WCR, LRR, CRR, URR and NRR. Each administrative area has its own social factors. Consequently I would like to take a political journey in each administrative area to determine what are the needs and concern of peoples living. The seven local administration authorities have very minimal autonomy. They are directly answerable to central government through the minister of local government, lands and regional chiefs; however, they are tasked with tax collection and other municipal duties. The head of each administration area is called the governor. In the first republic they used to be called commissioners: except for the Mayor of Banjul and the Mayor of KMC, all other heads of administration are called governors.

Let's start with the Banjul administrative area

Banjul is the capital city of the Gambia. The city, formerly called Bathurst, is at the mouth of the river Gambia. The administrative authority in the city is the Banjul City Council (BCC). The head of the administration is the Mayor of Banjul. A large proportion of city residents are Wolof or people who speak the Wolof language. Apart from modern sports, there are very few youth activities in Banjul. The Wolof language is the business language of the Gambia. However, Wolof and non-Wolof co-exist peacefully, and inter-marriage is common. There are no forests, no factories, no farmers, and no vegetable gardens in Banjul. There are only a few empty areas remaining in the city, with no bush except a little jungle near the river. The economy of Banjul is totally dependent on commerce, visitors from outside Banjul, and office work. The city is full of government administration buildings, including the famous State House, the official residence of the president of the republic; the central bank of the Gambia, the high court, police headquarters, the National Assembly building, the Mile 2 prison, the seaport and much more. The ferry terminal on the river bank is the connection between Banjul and the north bank region. However, there are still a few rented private properties as well as private residential areas in the city. During the official working hours of 8 a.m. to 4 p.m. the city is full of people coming from outside Banjul for work and business. The market, the schools and the main hospital of the country in Banjul are overcrowded. The hospital used to be called the Royal Victoria Hospital (RVH); but it's now called Edward Francis Small Teaching Hospital; and the headquarters of the major banks in the country are all located in the city. There are very few youth centres, sport venues and children's playgrounds in the city.

The environment and social challenges which face the city of Banjul

Sea erosion threatens the very existence of the city, as well as the city's environmental sustainability. There are poor road conditions and generally the infrastructure in the city is getting worse. Most buildings in the city are old. Gradually, the city is failing to attract investors. As a result most families are now leaving Banjul for other cities in the country. A lack of water drainage increases the alarming number of mosquitoes, especially during the night, and the period of the rainy season. During the summer the streets are running with water.

According to IEC electoral records, which might be useful for any potential candidate who may want to win the hearts and minds of Banjulians, Banjul has three constituencies. The total number of registered voters recorded in the Banjul North constituency is 7102, in Banjul South is 6258 and in Banjul Central is 9371. The number of registered voters living in Banjul is 22731.

Now it's up to you to do some homework and determine what rhetoric would you use to be elected in Banjul.

Let's go on and examine the next administrative area.

The Kanifing Municipal Council (KMC) administrative area

The Kanifing Municipal Council used to be called Kombo St. Mary Municipal Division (KSMD). The administrative authority of KMC is headed by the Mayor of KMC. By the share of population, it's the largest administrative area in the country. The major commercial city in the Gambia, Serrekunda, is the administrative capital of KMC. The administrative area includes tens of thousands of foreigners, hotel industries, factories, many government administrative buildings, clinic and hospitals, hundreds of schools, supermarkets and foreign embassies. KMC is culturally diverse; the inhabitants speak many languages, including at least ten indigenous languages. The KMC administrative area has the most robust infrastructure in the whole country; the area is very attractive to all kinds of investors and the population is growing more than anywhere else in the country. Every year thousands of peoples migrate from other administrative areas, particularly from rural areas, to relocate to the KMC. There are thousands of hectares of individual vegetable gardens, as well as small farming communities; however, in this area there is very little dependence on livestock.

It's also the home to many religious centres such as Muslim mosques and Christian churches with thousands of worshippers every day. KMC is the most attractive tourist destination in the Gambia, with easy access to the river Gambia and the Atlantic Ocean. The area's economy is mainly based on commerce, industry, manual physical labour, farming, and tourism. The famous independent stadium in Bakau is situated in KMC; there are many other youth football playgrounds in the area. Physical sport is very attractive to youths in the region. However there are fewer youth and community centres in the KMC.

The environmental and social challenges which face the KMC

Housing, sea erosion, mobility, communications and overcrowding are the challenges. KMC has a poor land record-keeping system; as a result there are frequent disputes over land and property. It has poor rubbish collection and a lack of water drainage system especially during the rainy reason. The rapid increase of land and housing prices is a major concern for many families. This is mainly due to the increased migration from rural areas to urban areas, which is driving the rising cost of living in the area. Social mobility is almost impossible in the area due to lack of job opportunities for youth; their migrating to Europe is a common occurrence.

Poor road condition has put constraints on communication and access to essential services like hospitals, schools and major commercial industries. Frequent water and electricity shortages are a common occurrence in the area. Anti-social behaviour and petty crime is dramatically declining; however, the underlying issues which cause crime and anti-social behaviour are slowly emerging. These include illicit drugs use, cannabis use, gambling, and alcohol abuse. There is inadequate security in the area which put constraints on security forces as well as the fire service.

According to the IEC records, the KMC has seven constituencies. The total amount of registered voters recorded in the Bakau constituency is 17148, in Jeshwang is 31857, in Serrekunda West is 4652, in Serrekunda central is 14701 in Serrekunda Bunduga Kunda is 31065, in Latrikunda Sabijie is 33970 and in Tallinding Kunjang is 24714. The total amount of registered voters in the KMC administrative area is 199957.

Now that you have the some details of the KMC, if you wanted to participate in the election in the KMC administrative area what political rhetoric would you use to attract communities to vote for you?

Let's proceed to another administrative area.

The West Coast Region (WCR)

The WCR, which used to be called Brikama Western Division, by size, is the largest administrative area in the Gambia. Brikama is the administrative capital of the WCR. There are many districts in the region. Brikama area council BCC is the administrative authority in the region, headed by the governor. The area's population is mainly dominated by Mandinka, as well as Jola and Fulla. Additionally the WCR is home to many other ethnic groups who speaks different languages and have a different culture. The inhabitants of the area co-exist peacefully and inter-marriage between ethnic tribes is common practice. In the WCR there are very few factories or industries, and fewer government administrative buildings. The economy of the area depends on farming, small business, arts, women's vegetable gardens, and animal breeding and livestock. In the whole country, it's the leading area for women vendors, as well as female ownership of business and land. Community diversity is increasing in the area.

The WCR is the second most attractive area for internal

41

migration; scores of families are migrating from other administrate areas. Educational institutions, health, and community services are also increasing in the area. According to police records there is less anti-social behaviour and crime recorded in the area. There is no shortage of sport grounds and playgrounds in the region and the area's youths are very active in physical sports as well as entertainment. Migration to Europe is common in the area. The residential buildings in the WCR and the street layouts are all from an earlier time. WCR is the second most attractive area for tourism and fishing. From most parts of the region you can easily get access to a large part of the river Gambia and the Atlantic Ocean. The former president Yahya Jammeh comes from the region. He was born on 25th May 1965 in a small village called Kanilai in a district of the Foni Kansala constituency. Let's check the challenges facing the region.

The environmental and social challenges facing the WCR

The WCR is facing with many urgent environmental and economic social challenges. Youth unemployment is among the biggest problems in the region and population growth is getting out of hand. There is very little proper infrastructure development, e.g. roads, communication, water and electricity supply. The region does not have enough schools and hospitals. With lack of a proper record keeping system, land and property dispute is a common occurrence in the area. Farmers in the region are in constant argument with domesticated animal owners. However there are no records of tribal conflict, or vengeance among the tribes living in the region.

According the IEC records from the last election, the WCR has the largest proportion of all registered voters in the Gambia. The KMC has more people than the WCR but a high proportion of them are foreigners who, by the constitution, are not allowed to vote. The WCR has twelve constituencies. The total amounts of registered voters recorded in the Foni Jarrol constituency is 3926, in Foni

Brefet is 8455, in Foni Bintang is 9073, in Foni Bondali is 4104, in Foni Kansala is 8245, in Kombo East is 21626, in Kombo South is 45152, in Brikama North is 29369, in Brikama South is 30814, in Sanneh Mentering is 39618, in Old Yundum is 44131, and in Busumbala is 36602. The total amount of registered voters recorded in WCR is 28115.

If you are someone with an intention to contest the election in this region, do your homework and determine what political rhetoric you would use to give you the keys to the State House.

Let's jump to the next administrative area.

The Lower River Region (LRR)

The LRR used to be known as the Lower River Division, and it is the region where I come from. My home town is called Sutukung, situated in the far east of the region close to the border with the CRR. The regional administrative capital is Mansa Konko and the head of the administration is the governor. As I stated earlier the local administration authorities have very minimal autonomy. There are directly answerable to central government through the Minister of local government lands and regional chiefs. The local authority in the region is Mansa Konko area council. Most people in the LRR live in the towns and villages. Mandinka people are the majority in the region, as well as Fulla and Sarahul; inter-marriage between tribes is not widespread like Banjul, KMC and WCR.

However, ethnic groups and local tribes are living peacefully side by side. The old fashioned Islamic education systems such as Majilis and Marabout teachers are common. There are fewer modern Madarashe schools, and fewer English schools. Most people in the region preferred to live by their culture and tradition; but, they are willing to subscribe to the common laws of the land, including Islamic laws. 30% of the LRR economy is coming from foreign aid via the support of families and friends living in the Diaspora; 25% is coming from farming and 20% coming from manual jobs. Fishing

43

and physical labour is not attractive to the region's population. There are almost no factories, no industries, and no tourist attractions in the area. There are many families depending on livestock. Vegetable gardens, animal farms, and fruit agriculture are common in the region. The forest is mostly covered by bush with few wild animals and birds. Youths in the LRR are actively engaging in physical sports and traditional wrestling. There are no community centres or children's playgrounds. The area is well known for annual traditional and religious ceremonies including youth vestals.

The social and environmental challenges which face the LRR

The social challenges facing the LRR are many. 15% of all Gambian youths who migrate to Europe via the risky 'back way' route via the Mediterranean Sea are from the LRR. Unemployment is rife in the area; most families are depending on outside support, usually from family and friends in the Diaspora. Deforestation is rapidly destroying the bush, exacerbated by bush fires. Tree planting and gardening are not desirable to many in the region; however, that is mainly due to the environmental difficulty of fertilising the land. The intellectual development is very slow is the area. Most inhabitants are still firmly holding on to the ancient belief which makes it a taboo to embrace and equip with modern intellectual tools. There are still significant numbers of people in the region who believe in witchcraft, evil spirits and myths, in contrast to Banjul, KMC, and WCR where such beliefs have perished. However, social segregation of peoples perceived by society as lower class is gradually disappearing with modern civilization, in contrast to CRR, NBR, and URR where such a practice is still prevalent.

According to IEC records from the last election, the LRR has six constituencies; the total amounts of voters registered in the Jarra West constituency is 14941, in the Jarra East constituency is 8609, in Jarra Central is 4820, in Kiang West is 10343, in Kiang East is 4483; and in Kiang Central is 6002. The total amount of voters registered in the LRR region is

49198. I really make your homework easy for you, if you want to steal the hearts of voters in the LRR.

Before we continue with our political journey to explore another administrative region (which is a very hot region and you might need to take a bottle of cold water with you) let's take a break while I share a ridiculous story with you. Please don't think I am an idiot if I start to sound like am contradicting myself. It's normal in African politics to contradict ourselves: it's the continent where often we dance and clap for our leaders in the morning and run after their motorcade with euphoria; we subsequently hate them in the evening and eventually send them to exile forever.

My friends used to wonder during the 2016 US presidential election campaign why I supported Donald Trump. They based their argument on the fact that Trump is claimed to have racist tendencies and misogynistic behaviour towards women. My response to them was always that I don't support Trump's view; neither do I support his anti-social behaviour. There are only two things which I liked about Trump's campaign. First his rhetoric ("Make America Great Again") and secondly, when Trump speaks, he talks like Trump: he never pretends to be someone else.

The logic behind my two points is: beforehand Donald Trump has done his homework to know exactly the main political dilemmas facing the USA. He came to realise that most citizens in the US don't feel great because a black man in the White House does not truly represent the US interest. People were yearning for a white man in the White House. He seized that opportunity and told them "Look, I am an upper-class white man, I know what you want; I promise I can make you feel great again." Amazingly, without a fight, they gave him the keys to the White House. That is political genius, isn't it? I wonder why people argue why I supported the actions of a political genius. We must give him credit for that.

My second point is this. Whenever Trump speaks, he talks

like Trump. He neither copies anyone nor does he sound like another politician. Trump is Trump, he has a unique political styles and it rewards him with success. How long that will last is a matter of debate for another day. No matter what, we must feel comfortable in our own skin and be ourselves, it's only that which will give us success.

If you are following my political journey, don't just follow, but learn from it and do your homework. Trust me, it works for Trump, and I am sure it would work for you.

Let's examine the CRR region.

Central River Division (CRR)

The CRR used to be known as Georgetown or McCarthy Island Division. Janjanbureh is the administrative capital of the CRR. There are many districts in the region. The head of the administration is the governor and the Janjanbureh area council is the local administrative authority in the region. Fulla people are the majority in the area as well as Mandinka, Wolof and Sarahul. Significant amounts of the population live in the old fashioned villages and small towns. So far no progress is been made on infrastructure development in the region. By a rough estimate only 25% of the land is built on or used for agricultural purposes. The rest of the lands are forest, full of wild life and superstition. The western part of the region is the home to the old fashioned Islamic schools, the Majilis learning centres and their Marabout teachers living close by (much like the LRR). There are fewer Arabic and English schools; however the second major hospital in the country is situated at Basang in the region. There are clinics and small health centres in the area. The culture of the area is similar to the URR which is next door to the CRR; a significant proportion of people are living by use of livestock. Apart from that, the life of about 35% of the people depend on farming, 20% depend on foreign remittance via the support of families and friends living in the Diaspora, and 25% depend on manual labour. Fishing and arts are attractive to the population. There are very few administrative buildings in the region. Like the LRR it's desirable for most people to live by their tradition and culture while at the same time respecting the rule of law and Islamic laws.

Yet the social conservative view is more widespread in the area than in the LRR. Inter-marriage to other tribes is slowly emerging among the younger generation but it's not widespread. Like its sister regions, youth unemployment has affected the area the most; thus a majority of youths has either migrated to urban areas to look for jobs or tried to use the 'back way' to Europe. The CRR is one of the leading areas in the country where women are very active working on agriculture farms, vegetable gardens and animal breeding; the region is very famous for domesticated animal farmers including those living in the forest. Annual religious ceremonies and traditional festivals are common. Wrestling and traditional music is still prevalent in the area; the area's youths participate in all kinds of sports and entertainment.

The administrative capital Janjanbureh is very famous for the Kankurang festivals; there is an interesting legend behind that. In honour of that festival, the National Centre for Art and Culture built a history museum in town and named the building the Kankurang Centre. The CRR has many small islands which can only be accessed by boat or ferry. Armitage High School and the McCarthy prison made the town of Janjanbureh very famous, as have the Wassu stone circles in the region.

The social and environmental challenges facing the CRR

The CRR is the second hottest area in the Gambia, yet there has been no significant progress made to tackle the electricity problem in the region. Migration to urban areas from the region is another headache. Agriculture, which used to be the backbone of the economy, is gradually failing; animal thieves operating in the area have made it very difficult for animal breeders, and particularly cattle farmers. The relationship between the different tribes living in the region could be better. Sea erosion and deforestation is causing problems in the area as well as lack of tourist attractions. The segregation of people perceived as lower class is endemic in the region: in some places they use different graveyards for different social classes. It's almost impossible for one social class to marry another social class, in contrast to Banjul, KMC, WCR and LRR. However, a similar practice is very common particularly in the highlands of the CRR, the central districts of the NBR and the eastern districts of the URR.

The former President Jawara comes from the CRR; he stated his book *Kairaba* that he was born on 16th May 1924 in a small village called Barajaly in a district of the Niani constituency. But his government failed to introduce civic education to tackle that culture of social segregation as well as the harmful traditions which affect the society in the region. Anti-social behaviour is not yet an issue for the CRR; however, the underlying issues which cause anti-social behaviours are common in the region, e.g. drug trafficking and theft. The western part of the region such as Niamina is well known for wild speculation and bizarre stories of evil spirits controlling some aspects of the forest, the bush and even people's property. Visitors are regularly advised to be careful of spirits in the region. Some peoples even warn against any form of excessive worship of God in the area which they claim could bring "negative consequences". Such a concept in not confined to the region alone, it is a widespread belief throughout the nation. Malaria is the main cause of death in the Gambia, and in particular in the CRR. The high proportion of mosquitoes in the region has been a cause of concern for some time now; yet the government is not making enough effort to tackle that.

For any potential future politicians, this is how the IEC registers the CRR: the region has eleven constituencies. The total amounts of people registered to vote in the Janjanbureh constituency is 1980; in Niani is 13593, in Nianja is 4974, in Niamina West is 4375, in Niamina East is 11151, in Niamina Dankunku is 3547, in Lower Fulladu West is 20414, in Upper Fulladu West is 24678, in Lower Saloum is 9253, in Upper

Saloum is 11042 and in Sami is 11641. The total number of people registered to vote in the CRR region is 116675. As a politician; you must your time and do a case study of each region in the country beforehand. Surely, come the election, it would work out in your favour.

Before we cross the border to the URR, it's time for another observation.

Did you realise as a politician you have to familiarise yourself with different peoples customs, culture tradition and religion before you can approach to ask for their votes? The more you know about society, the more chance you have to win their trust. Initially good politicians strive to educate their citizens in order to save them from self-destruction and harmful practices; in the end leaders are revered and people worship them. However, by contrast, a bad politician capitalises on people's ignorance and uses it to their advantage. When people wake up from their long sleep and realise they have been taken for a ride by their leaders, they start to hate their political leaders. In the end they will throw the leader's legacy in the rubbish bin.

The slow progress on intellectual development of Gambians is hindering the citizen's ability to hold their government accountable. If Gambia had political intellectuals like Hon. Halifa Sallah in the past, the country would be intellectually greater today. Halifa has not only restored citizens' confidence in their own citizenship, but equally he restored the credibility of the Gambian constitution, and continues to fight and defend the reputation of the Constitution from being ruined. I call him the adopted child of the constitution.

Many major institutions in the country are run by foreign nationals; this includes judges in courts rooms, teachers at the schools, and business tycoons behind the import and export industries. Most factories as well as hotels are either owned by foreigners or being run by them. The majority of teachers in the Gambian secondary schools, high schools, colleges, and the University of the Gambia are all foreigners: those teachers mostly come from Nigeria, Ghana, Sierra Leone and elsewhere. Thus when most Gambian students speak English, they usually sound like foreigners. Lately I noticed one peculiar behaviour common among youths: when they speak English, they have an American accent. I cannot quite work out why that is. Perhaps they imitate actors and actresses from the US film industry, who are well known in Africa. If politicians keep on preaching to the citizens about good governance and accountability without intellectually addressing the issue, there will be no meaningful progress. Intellectual citizens means political leaders will realise their subjects are not a bunch of losers and idiots and they will think twice before committing any sort of crime.

The Upper River Region (URR)

Basse, in the URR, is the officially the second capital of the Gambia. The region used to be known as the Upper River Division. Basse is the administrative centre of the area, with many districts. Basse area council is the administrative authority in the region, led by the governor. Basse fails to attract major investors like banks, hotels, manufacturing companies and tourism, thus the town struggles to attain city status. However, there are many government administration buildings situated in the town, plus banks, schools and the community centre. Via Basse it's easy to get access to neighbouring countries like Senegal and Guinea Conakry.

The essential institutions such as high schools, major hospitals, communication centres and commercial industries are gradually improving in the area. According to a rough estimate 40% of the area's economy comes from farming, 30% comes from commerce and industry, and 25% comes from foreign remittance via the support of family and friends from abroad. Admin jobs, manual labour, and arts are not very common in the area. Most people in the region engage in small business, commerce and livestock services.

Social life and norms in the area very much resemble the CRR. The community in the region is very diverse, the majority of which speaks Mandinka, Fulla, and Sarahul. Most people in the area considered themselves to be social conservatives and prefer to lives by their local culture and ancient tradition. The largest share of the Jah-hankah community living in the Gambia is residing in the region. Jahkah is my own ethnic group; they are mainly residing in the LRR, CRR and URR. As I have stated in my first book Marriage and Society, Jah-hankah people are the sub-ethnic group belonging to Mandinka tribes. To refer to them as an ethnic group is more correct terminology than a tribe.

Except for the Jola (who are mainly settling in the greater Banjul area and the WRC), the area has all the other tribes peacefully co-existing without experiencing any major tribal difficulties.

Yet deep rooted cultures which created social segregation like negative social lower and upper class system is a very common occurrence in the region, similar to the CRR and NBR as I described earlier. The current president Adama Barrow comes from this region. He was born on 15th February 1965 in a small village called Mankamang Kunda in the Jimara constituency. Roughly only 30% of the lands in the area are built on; the rest is forest and farming land. The area is also home to more wildlife than the rest of the country. The river Gambia surrounds many parts of the region, with many small islands. The weather is very hot particularly during the rainy season. 35% of all youths travel to Europe through the 'back-way' due to youth unemployment. The area's youths are very active in physical sports and traditional entertainments. Urban migration is slowly affecting the progress of area population growths. Traditional Islamic Majilis are popular in the region as are Marabout institutions, plus annual religious ceremonies and indigenous traditional festivals.

The challenges facing the URR

These are mostly social and environmental difficulties, similar to the CRR. Bad transport and road communication, clean water shortages as well as lack of rural electricity extension are among the major problems in the region. The area is lagging behind in the intellectual development of children. Let's check the IEC electoral records for the region.

The URR has seven constituencies. The total amount of people registered to vote in the Basse constituency is 20655, in Jimara is 21434, in Tumana is 16966, in Kantora is 19146, in Sandu is 13167, in Wulli West is 11632 and in Wulli East is 12185. The total amount of people registered to vote in the URR is 115185.

I have done the research for you: now do your homework. After a final break we will continue our political journey to reach our final destination, which is the NBR.

I am going to share another story with you. It's slightly different from our main subjects but the story is relevant to Gambian politics. I just need to highlight the hypocrisy of western foreign policy towards Africa. Do you remember a few weeks ago, the UNDP and EU released a joint statement in relation to FGM and homosexual rights laws in the Gambia; According to the joint statement, these two institutions expect the new Gambia government to keep the law which banned female genital mutilation; while at the same time advising the new Gambian government to reverse other laws which came to force during the Jammeh era particularly laws which are against homosexual rights in the country.

My take on this: why can't the new government reverse every single law which was enforced by Jammeh's administration upon the nation and let the national assembly deliberate on them, to determine which laws are good for the country and which are bad. I think that makes more sense than a double standard.

If you recall back in the summer of 2003 when St Therese's secondary school at Westfield banned pupils from wearing the Muslim veil, it created a big noise which nearly set the country on fire. At the time I backed the decision of the school. Basically my argument was that the school is a

Christian missionary school. If the rules don't allow Muslim student wearing a Muslim symbol at their school, what is wrong with that? If any Muslim student wants to wear the Muslim veil, let them go to Muslim school elsewhere and wear it there. Female students who were insisting on wearing the veil in school didn't usually wear it outside school life. That was pure hypocrisy on their part.

The North Bank Region (NBR)

The NRR used to be known as the North Bank Division. Kerewan is the regional capital of the area; and Kerewan area council is the administrative authority in the region. The governor is the head of administration there. Like the other six regions in the country, there are many small districts in NBR. The AFPRC general hospital in Farafenni is the most famous building in the region. Admin buildings are fewer than most administrative areas in the country. However the area is very popular for the neighbouring Senegal people, particularly those close to the border, who would usually do all their shopping there. Mandinka people are the majority in the area, as well as Fulla, Wolof and Serere. Other ethnic minority groups are living peacefully among them.

The region is surrounded by the river Gambia but there are no small islands. Marriage between different tribes is not common. Almost 45% of the region's economy is coming from farming and livestock; 40% is coming from foreign remittance via the supports of families and friends from abroad. 10% is coming from fishing and small businesses. Arts and manual labour are not attractive to many people in the area. Most people desire to live by their own culture and tradition, however like other six regions in the country they subscribe to the other laws of the land, including Muslim laws. Compared to the LRR, URR and CRR, traditional Marabout schools are fewer in the region, due to being replaced by English and well as Arabic schools. Apart from the AFPRC general hospital in Farafenni, there are only a handful of clinics and health centres in the region.

Scores of schools, roads and bridges were built in the NBR by the APRC regime. Most people are living in densely populated villages and small towns, usually in old fashioned buildings. Livestock and animal breeding is widespread in the region. In some districts of the NBR, women are very actively working in vegetable gardens and other farming. Nearly 60% of the forest is empty of wildlife and human inhabitants. The area's youths participate in all kind of sports and modern entertainment. There are fewer community centres and no playgrounds for children. Religious ceremonies are common in the area especially during the Gambian winter. The crime rate, including domestic violence, in the region is still below average.

The major challenges facing the NBR

Social challenges are the main ones in the region; e.g. rapid rural migration to urban areas which has affected the NBR more than any other region in the Gambia. Some villages and towns are almost completely deserted: most people who migrated from the region are now settling in the greater Banjul area and the WCR. Usually they engage in commerce and small business as well manual labour. Youth migration to Europe using the 'back way' has caused nearly 18% of the area's youths to leave. Social segregation has affected the area. In some extreme cases, the community uses a different cemetery for burial for each social class, as in the CRR and URR. The area faces the same environmental challenges as the rest of the country.

Finally let's focus on the IEC records for the region. The NBR has seven constituencies. The total amount of people registered to vote in the Lower Nuimi constituency is 23935, in Upper Nuimi is 14536, in Jokadu is 10725, in Lower Baddibu is 9672, in Illiasa is 20826 and in Sabach Sanjal is 12241. The total amount of people registered to vote in the NBR is 101717.

As we approach the end of our political journey, it's crucial to critique the factors of each region in order to reach to a satisfactory conclusion. I can guarantee you that all the social factors I list for each region are not based on hypothetical circumstances or a biased political opinion. For the six months before and after the election, my charity work with the "Back to School Foundation" took me the length and breadth of the country to see for myself the social and environmental factors of the Gambia.

Thus the information I gather does not come from a political researcher's point of view. As a charity worker, when I meet individuals and communities, they feel confidence to willingly share their personal stories with me, and express their genuine concerns.

The information from each administrative area has come from my own perspective. However, later on I will share some vital information with you which was gathered from the Gambia Bureau of Statistics.

The figures on the economic and environmental factors which I have calculated and indicated in a percentage form were based on the number of people I spoke to; therefore it might be slightly different from the data of other agencies, particularly the UNPD and the Gambia Bureau of Statistics. Government-sponsored research and individual research sometimes varies.

When I approached the Gambia Bureau of Statistics for data relating to the percentage of each tribe leaving in every region, as well as who are the majority tribes in the Gambia, I was told that the Bureau has accurate data in relation to that, however due to the politically sensitive situation in the country the Bureau is not willing to share that data with the public, since it might trigger some unscrupulous individuals to use that as a weapon against minority tribes and other ethnic groups in the country.

For me that is absolutely the truth. I agreed with them on that 100% and equally I respected all precautionary measures by the Bureau to tackle that. Consequently, I decided not to publish the percentage of the rough figures I gather about the share of each tribe in every region. Probably when the political atmosphere is lot calmer in the country I could publish those details in a future edition.

However, it's important to highlight the following factors. English is the official language in the Gambia but in the greater Banjul area, KMC and WCR, most people speak Wolof because it is the business language of the country. In the LRR, CRR, URR and NBR, most people speak Wolof, Mandinka and Fulla. It's essential to bring this to your attention: there is an 80% cultural similarity between all tribes and ethnic groups in the country.

For an example, early marriage affected all tribes in the Gambia; female genital mutilation also affects most tribes in the country, and the children from all tribes faces the same social and economic challenges. The deep rooted culture of social stratification which created segregation against a particular social class in the society is widespread in all communities. Cultural similarities to other areas in the country are common in the urban areas too (the Greater Banjul area, KMC and WCR). In those areas you can still notice at least 20% of the culture is very similar to those from other regions in the country. This is usually due to migration: when people migrate, they migrate with their culture. The following summary came from the Gambia Bureau of Statistics.

"The Gambia was ruled by the British for two centuries; it became self-governing in 1963, and gained full independence on 18th February 1965. The country became a sovereign republic in 1970 with maintenance of multiparty democracy, adherence to the rule of law and preservation of fundamental human rights and integral parts of the country's political framework.

The Gambia is located midway on the bulge of the West African coast and stretches over 400 kilometres from west to east on either side of the River Gambia, varying in width from about 50 km near the mouth of the river, to about 24 km upstream. The country is bounded to north, south, and east by the republic of Senegal and to the west by the Atlantic

Ocean. The river Gambia, which runs the entire length of the country from the Futa Jallon highlands in the republic of Guinea to the Atlantic Ocean, divides the country's land area of 10,689 square kilometres almost equal into half: the south bank and the north bank.

The Gambian climate is typically Sahelian with a long dry season from November to May and a short rainy season between June and October. The estuary basin of the River Gambia is virtually a tidal inlet with salt water intrusion ranging from 180 km upstream in the rainy season to 250 km in the dry season. Irrigable land area is limited, and therefore agriculture which is the backbone of the Gambian economy, is mostly rain fed. As a result, agricultural activities are subject to wide seasonal fluctuations and production levels are vulnerable to variations in rainfall.

The economy has a market based economy characterised by traditional subsistence agriculture and a significant tourist industry. The world bank estimates the 2012 gross domestic product GDP in the Gambia at $944 million(current prices) and $707 million(constant prices) the services sector continues to be the leading contributor to the GDP. Agriculture accounted for roughly 22 percent of the GDP in 2012 and 2013, and this sector employs about 70 percent of the labour force.

The population is 1.9 million, 50 percent of them residing in the rural area, and women constitute 51 percent of total population. The total fertility rate is 5.4 births per woman. This high fertility level has resulted in a very youthful population structure. Almost 65 percent of population are youths and young peoples. 96 percent of population are Muslims whiles the rest are Christian and other religious minority group; sources; the Gambia Bureau of Statistic Demographic and health survey 2013".

Most Muslims in the Gambia are liberal; however, there are still significant amount of Muslims who consider themselves as conservative.

The only thing missing from this report is how many people belong to each political party in each region as a percentage; as I stated before, in the Gambia in particular, which tribe you belong to and the ethnic background you come from as well as the region you originated from are the crucial factors in African politics.

With the wealth of information I have provided for you, let's collectively test the ability of our understanding and go back to the central topic, which is rhetoric and political slogans. After reading this book, if you are a Gambian politician who is interested to contest the election in the Gambia in 2017, what would be your political rhetoric?

Are you going to use the rhetoric of Tony Blair ("Education, education, education"), or would it be Barack Obama's "Yes We Can" or perhaps Donald Trump's "Let's Make America [Gambia] Great Again"?

Guess what? None of the above would presently work for you in the Gambia. If I was going to participate at any election in the Gambia on any political party ticket, guess what my rhetoric would be?

"Say No To Dictatorship Again".

This rhetoric and a party manifesto based on it will massively resonate with the overwhelming majority of Gambian voters, because it will give them much needed assurance. Surly they would vote for me! 22 years of dictatorship in the Gambia has affected every single Gambian in one way or another: even president Yahya Jammeh has been affected by it. It's because of dictatorship that he could no longer stay in the Gambia to be a farmer at his farms in Kanilai, as he has previously wished.

At the moment, dictatorship is the talk of the town. People's minds are still fresh about it. As I stated earlier, for any politician to make impacts in the electoral process you have to capitalise on the issues which matter the most to the public, including the use of slogans from the main topic in town. During the late 2016 presidential election campaign, it's not the members of the Coalition but their supporters who created their own slogan in Mandinka when referring to president Jammeh: "AYE-GI-AYE-GI-AYE-GI" which simply means "Get down, get down, get down". Amazingly it worked.

Also during the political stalemate, another effective slogan began to surface in town #GAMBIA HAS DECIDED which was printed in the front of white-shirts and distributed among coalition supporters, as well as written on banners and posters.

We should remember that during any political campaign in any country at any time, rhetoric and slogan are very effective tools which give the key to success; however, different times mean different issues, different rhetoric and different slogans.

Using political slogans to win the elections is only one small aspect of moving the country forwards. The social challenges and economic factors which you have learnt from this book in relation to Gambian society will help you to build the Gambia to attain economic super-power status in Africa.

Think back to the late 1990s when President Jawara promised to build the Gambia economically to become like Singapore: he failed. In the late 2000's President Jammeh constantly promised he would build the Gambia to become like Dubai but he failed too. Why was that? In my opinion to build the Gambia to attain the economic super-power status in Africa will start right at the schools, all the way to the courts. The country does not only need intellectuals, but genuine intellectuals. I will give some very good examples.

Back in summer 2014, when I was in Sydney, Australia, as Ebola was engulfing West Africa, I read in the one Gambian newspaper that a reputable Imam in the Gambia gave a Friday sermon in the Mosque in which he stated that Ebola was punishment from God due to our sins. Amazingly people started believing in it. I was not only puzzled by the Imam's bizarre claim, but I was equally disappointed in the reputable newspaper which published the sermon. Can you imagine the mind-set behind such claims? Such remarks from the Imam in the mosque and Pastors from the church is an open invitation to unscrupulous societies who might want to test lethal chemicals; they could easily target Africa, bearing in mind that when things go wrong, the public will consider it as punishment from God. There are too many conspiracy theories surrounding the cause of Ebola and HIV AIDS: before people make such wild claims, they should wait for local scientists to thoroughly investigate the matter. It's common for some minority religious people to assume that the whole point of being an Imam is to strike fear in people's hearts and minds and strike terror into their daily lives.

In 2009, some people in the Gambia praised President Jammeh when he ordered the arrest of suspected witches in Foni and Kombo for their so-called involvement in witchcraft which it was claimed resulted in the deaths of some of his former aides. He was capitalising on public ignorance.

Basically my argument is this: you cannot build any country to attain the economic super-power status if the citizens are ill-equipped with logic and rational thinking.

Note: last year in the Kingdom of Saudi Arabia; the minister responsible for housing was ridiculed on Twitter, when he Tweeted one of the sayings of the prophet; which stated that you should "love your neighbour even if they are bad to you". Almost 40,000 people in Saudi replied to his Tweet by telling him to look after the affairs of state and leave the preaching to Islamic scholars (my source: the Gulf News). Currently Saudi Arabia is the leading country in the Gulf region who is giving scholarship to almost 70,000 citizens to study various disciplines, mainly in Europe, Australia, New Zealand and the USA, in order to properly intellectually equip them. While I was in Auckland, New Zealand, in 2013 I meet many such students who benefited from that pilot scheme.

Each citizen should have the ability to raise their concerns to their political and religious leaders when they fail to perform their duties to the nation. In early February 2017, Gambian students protested outside the National Assembly building in Banjul to demand the resignation of all members in the house for the role they played in extending the mandate of former President Jammeh, as well as their own mandate, for three months during the impasse. The culture of the Gambian National Assembly for not properly holding the government accountable surfaced again on 26th February 2017, when the Minister of the Interior tabled the bill in the House before

NAMs which would extend the age limits for presidential candidate, vice-president, and chief justice from 65 years. According to Hon. Halifa Sallah, that bill was passed without properly following the due process of the constitution. Can you imagine: within the first two months of the coalition government, such failure to properly follow the procedures according to the constitution has occurred at least three times? It happened to the change of NIA to SIS, the appointment of the vice president who whose age was above the limit at the time of her appointment, as well as the National Assembly endorsing the age limit bill. It vindicated my previous point where I indicated that due to our Gambian culture, citizens at all levels do not usually have the appetite to oppose the government if they are wrong.

I should say, if you notice, most of the time I refer to Jawara and Jammeh as "President" rather than addressing them as "former President". In that, I follow the tradition of the USA who always referred to their former leaders as President Clinton, President Bush and so on. I think, it's really important for us as Africans to observe due respect to all our leaders, no matter how they left office. In the United Kingdom, when addressing their former Kings and Queens; always they referred to them as King so and so and Queens so and so, not 'former'. Another important observation is: I touched on every aspect of President Jammeh's public life, however, I didn't mention anything about his private life apart from mentioning the names of his spouse on a few occasions. Under any circumstances, we should leave people's private life as private, no matter how controversial it is.

For me I am really proud to share my personality with President Jawara, share my first name with President Jammeh and my hobby in reading with President Adama Barrow; I am looking forward to share something interesting with the next President of the republic of the Gambia.

CHAPTER 4
THE PERIOD FROM THE 1996 ELECTION TO THE 2016 ELECTION

Two years after the coup, on Thursday 26th September 1996, the first presidential election was held and Yahya Jammeh easily won the election without a struggle. After the election, life seemed to be getting to back to normal in the Gambia. However, for Jammeh and his disciples, life was far from getting back to normal. There were constant rumours of Jammeh maintaining his grip on power by slowly getting rid of agitators within the army: close aides like Lt. Alimamo Manneh disappeared from the Gambia. The new civilian election was nothing other than window dressing; as Jammeh himself stated "once a military is always a military". He was 100% correct: for the next twenty years, the Gambia was ruled with a military styled iron fist.

The first national assembly election was held on 2nd January 1997, three months after the presidential election, as required by the constitution. The new assembly replaced the British style of parliament system, which referred to representatives as "members of parliament". The new representatives were called "members of the national assembly" (NAMs). They replaced the former House of Parliament who members used be called MPs. However, former MPs and current NAMs play the same role in the legislative body, which is crucial to the functions of the government and the country. This gentle and innocent assembly would soon find itself firmly in the passenger seat, while President Jammeh took control from the driving seat.

On Thursday 7th August 1997, hundreds of thousands of Gambians, including myself, overwhelmingly voted to endorse the newly drafted constitution; commonly known as the 1997 constitution. This important booklet would later become the most controversial book in Gambian history.

The APRC government, via the legislative members of the

national assembly, reduced the value of the 1997 constitution to that of a normal school exercise book. They constantly changed the content of the constitution as a primary school teacher changes a black board; just to serve their political agenda and the interests of the president and his executives.

Asa rough estimate, the 1997 constitution was amended at least 49 times by the office of the president and the national assembly, all serving to massively boost the muscular ego of Yahya Jammeh. During the 2016 political crisis in the Gambia, the 1997 constitution retained its value like the British pound sterling. Thanks to the IEC and Mr Halifa Sallah whom frequently drew the bases of their arguments against Jammeh and the APRC from it; as well as recommending that those who might doubt their story to go back to it and draw their own conclusions from it.

Apart from the holy Quran, in 2016, the 1997 constitution became the most read book in the Gambia. I can still vividly remember very well in late December 2016, many book shops across the Gambia ran out of copies due to high demand. It took me a whole week to get a new copy after I lost my first one. The constitution contained all the supreme laws of the Gambia. It was the important instrument for running the Gambian government, the country, and civil society. It was equal to that of the United States constitution. It replaced the military decrees which came into force after the coup. It was the second such constitution which came to existence in the Gambia following independence. The first constitution was written in 1971.

President Jammeh's government enjoyed almost a seven year period of political honeymoon before the average Gambian was critical of them. However, the shocking student massacre of April 10th-11th 2000 completely and dramatically broke that trust.

As I witness; I can still vividly remember the full drama as it occurred. It was 8 a.m. on Monday when I heard about an on-going student demonstration. As a curious excited man, I headed to Westfield and witnessed a public outcry of which I had never seen the like. While at Westfield, during the early stages of the demonstration, around 9:30 a.m., I saw the arrival of a significant amount of military men and women.

At first it was calm and peaceful; however, as the time approached midday, without warning it suddenly became deadly. The military and the Police fired teargas into the crowd several times without any effective result; at that stage I saw agitation and frustration on their faces. At one stage they fired tear gas towards us and it affected me so badly I started sneezing like I had the flu. I decided to go home, because at that moment, the situation was almost out of control. The Gamtel house situated at Westfield was set on fire. You could see the fire engulf the whole house and the surrounding buildings were at risk. On my way home, I decided to pass by Churches town. I saw the fire station there was also ablaze. The violent behaviour and the aggressive manner of the student demonstrators made me so worried, my instinct was that it was time to quickly run home. Without exaggeration the atmosphere was equal to a war zone. It was beyond belief. Can you imagine private property as well as government buildings burning to ashes; some student protestors started to loot any valuable items that they could lay their hand on. That was a step too far and what followed dramatically changed the relationship between Jammeh's government and Gambian citizens, from that day, right up to the end of his tenure.

I was thankful for the quick decision I made that day to quickly return home; it helps to compose me to share the horrors with you today in this noble book; especially after I heard the magnitude of the destruction of lives and property which occurred that day. However, my heart goes out to all victims that perished in that tragedy; particularly to their families and loved ones who still live with the loss and anguish.

I am not a legal expert or law practitioner but even I know it was it was not justifiable to take 16 innocent lives like that. Hopefully both sides, and the whole nation, have learnt a valuable lesson from it. As a civilised society; let's not repeat past mistakes and collectively turn the page to new chapter. For their part, the government should ensure freedom of expression is widely available for all citizens. The public should not abuse that privilege. Instead they must ensure whenever they exercise their freedom of expression it's done within the law without excessive damage to lives and property.

We must note that in April 2000, Gambian students were protesting to show their anger of the manner in which the security forces allegedly abused their colleagues in the previous weeks leading to the demonstration. There were claims that an officer from a paramilitary unit, while on duty at the Bakau independent stadium, raped a female student. Another student accused the men at Brikama fire station of forcing him to drink cement mixed with water as punishment for an alleged crime. Security forces dismissed both allegations as nonsense but as a result, the Gambia student union GAMSU organised the demonstration against the Gambian security forces.

For peaceful protest to escalate to lethal riots is a common occurrence around the world. A similar protest escalated to full riots in the United Kingdom on 6th-11th August 2011. Youths mainly from black and ethnic backgrounds were demonstrating to show their anger about the killing of Mark Duggan in police custody. Just few hours into a peaceful demonstration it escalated to violent riots across other English cities; consequently 5 people died and16 were injured as well as 186 police officers seriously sustained injuries. When the situation further escalated to more violence; the then Mayor of London Boris Johnson took some desperate measures including allowing the Metropolitan police to use any force which was necessary to put the end to riots, even if that meant using live ammunition against rioters.

In South Africa, from 10th-20th August 2012, miners at Marikana protested against their employers for a pay rise as well as improved working conditions. On 16th August 2012, the South African police force fired live ammunition against miners and subsequently killed 34, as well as seriously wounded hundreds of others; according to South Africa police department, some police officers also sustained serious injuries in the incident. Up to now, no one has been punished for this heinous crime.

In the year 2001 before the general election, Gambians were eagerly waiting to crucify the APRC government in the polls, as punishment for their involvement in the previous year's student massacre. However, President Jammeh and his government were one million steps ahead of the country. It would take the nation at least 15 more years to be rid of Jammeh.

The 2001 election was held on Thursday 18th October; President Jammeh decisively beat his main contender, lawyer Ousainou Darboe, the UDP presidential candidate. Just for your information, one year before that election I left the Gambia for the United Kingdom. Many stories which I relay from now on are second-hand information; mostly gathered from my friends in the Gambia, or Gambian citizens living in the United Kingdom.

According to sources, during the 2001 presidential campaign, Darboe was most political pundit's favourite to win the elections. However, dramatic events occurred late on election night. While the IEC continued to count and announce the election results across the country, barely before the count reached half of the popular vote, Darboe conceded defeat and called to congratulate His Excellency retired Colonel Dr Professor Alahaji Yahya AJJ Jammeh for his landslide victory. This amazes furious Darboe supporters to this day. They blamed him for easily handing over his smooth road to the State House to Jammeh. I still ask myself: what was the motive and philosophy behind what Darboe did? Was it due to intimidation of Darboe and his supporters by the military junta, or stress or perhaps inner pressure from within Darboe's own psychology? Whatever it was, such a move was counterproductive for the Gambia.

Note: From 1996 to 2016, the United Democratic Party was the main opposition political party in the Gambia. And they successfully managed to grow, whilst former main political parties such as the PPP, NCP and PDOIS became less influential. However, the NRP did their best to maintain the position of the second main political party in the country. They currently hold two national assembly seats. The Gambia currently has nine registered political parties in the country. Most of them have participated in the elections since from 1996-2016, occasionally in small coalitions. Seven of them, including one independent candidate, successfully formed the largest coalition ever and subsequently won the 2016 election against the incumbent Yahya Jammeh. Apart from the 2016 election, the 2001 election was the most contested election in the Gambia political history.

Did you know that Gambia is among the countries where a political party's manifesto and policy are not relevant to the geopolitical system? Political parties usually attract their supporters by using the influence of tribes and tribal leaders and by showing who is more willing to shower the population with cash. As I will state in Chapter Five; there is no common interest in the country or shared belief in ideas. For the past thirty years the People's Democratic Organization for Independence and Socialism (PDOIS) has been vigorously campaigning via their affiliated newspaper, the Froyaa news, which is providing information to educate people in relation to politics, civics and social justice. However so far they have managed to register very little success. The majority of the population are still holding to the old fashioned traditional belief systems i.e. under any circumstances you must stay loyal to leaders, elders, those in the position of authority and rulers at any level, even if they are lacking the moral capacity and ability to lead, because they are divinely chosen to play that role for society.

Consequently, opposition to the leaders and those occupying positions of authority are not desirable for most people in the Gambia. But with the increase of globalization and the increased use of social media such an attitude is slowly disappearing from the younger generations.

On Thursday 17th January 2002, the Gambia held its second national assembly election. By now Jammeh's ruling APRC party had taken full control of the national assembly. Only handful of opposition members managed to share the house floor with them. Baba Kajally Jobe delightedly sat in the chair of the national assembly as a majority leader and comfortably ran the show without any dispute from his compatriots; however, later in the following year, 2003, Jammeh would climb the ladder and bring him down as well as tear him apart. In just a few days, the banks and private businesses would all be closed, and the flamboyant lifestyle which came with it suddenly came to an end.

Meanwhile, Jobe's mates - the 'green boys' and the 22 July movement - were partying like there was no tomorrow, whilst pretending that no one was missing from the top spot. Mile 2 central prison would later gain the title of "Baba Jobe's hotel". Since then the camps of Jammeh and Baba Jobe asserted claim and counter-claim accusing one another like schoolboys fighting to date one famous girl.

At that stage Jammeh was not shy to show the international community that he was embracing the status of an old fashioned dictator. Without realizing, the Gambian army was merely reduced to Jammeh's personal army. Gambian civil servants would become champion farmers in Kanilai, not for their fathers, but for the President of the Republic. Before the next general election, Jammeh would assume the leadership of all major institutions in the Gambia. The running of the state was done by presidential directive and executive orders from the office of the president.

On Tuesday March 21st 2006, with Gambians preparing going to bed, the commander-in-chief of Gambia's armed forces, Colonel Ndrou Cham, and his followers, were cocking up a coup to overthrow Jammeh's government. The naive army chief completely failed to realize all the available luck in the land belonged to Jammeh and his henchmen. The coup mysteriously failed without a single shot being fired. At the eleventh hour, the colonel betrayed his followers when he became aware that Jammeh knew all his plans; nothing was heard from him from that day on. Since then many patriotic citizens disappeared without a trace. Jammeh's notorious national intelligent services would play a crucial role in consolidating his grip on power. Neighbouring Senegal soon became the home for Gambian dissidents.

Later in the same year on 2nd July 2006, the republic of the Gambia, under the dynamic leadership of President Yahya AJJ Jammeh Musa, successfully hosted the African union summit. Almost thirty heads of state and many foreign government officials attended. It was the first time Gambia ever hosted such an event.

On Friday 22nd September 2006, Gambians went to the polls for the third time in ten years to renew the mandate of President Jammeh. During the short campaign period, Jammeh used the sympathy card of the March failed coup attempt against him. It massively worked in his favour and gave him a landslide victory, despite the opposition of a coalition of four political parties. Meanwhile, the supporters of the opposition UDP were constantly criticising their party leader Ousainou Darboe for his lack of charisma and for not making any significant progress to democratically push Jammeh out of office.

Darboe is a very talented, measured, attentive and intelligent lawyer. He has successfully represented high profile individuals and influential people in the Gambian court, including politicians, businessmen, civil servants and farmers. By using his talent, he defended them and prevented many people from going to jail. His is not a stranger to the Gambian legal system and he is a well-respected man within the judiciary. However, in 1996 when he was chosen to lead the newly established UDP, the public expectation for him to quickly remove President Jammeh from power was monumental. But for Darboe, that journey would be equal to

Nelson Mandela's long walk to freedom. A legally minded person like Darboe, who only believes in the due process of law, was in complete contrast to the man opposite him who is a person who uses the mighty forces of the army as well as abiding to no rules except his own. For one to accomplish the task to remove that person from power would not only take luck, but a tremendous amount of sacrifice with many sleepless nights. It took ten years for the Gambian opposition to succeed in that, but in the meantime, Gambians were very impatient by the slow pace of Darboe's progress.

There are schools of thought that criticise Darboe's leadership style; their argument is that Darboe was extremely slow to develop his political skills and his public image. I have to admit, in late 2011, during the period of presidential election campaign, when I listened to Darboe on GRTS TV, compared to his political opponents I felt "discombobulated" with the manner of his public statements, which always sounded to me like a first time job interview of high school graduates. Often when he walked on stage or gave a public speech, he came across more like a lawyer in the courtroom than a politician in the public domain. He couldn't make jokes with his audience even when they were his supporters. And usually when he spoke, his settled tone and soft voice didn't bring much joy and excitement to the public like, say, Yahya Jammeh or Hamat Bah, the leader of the NRP, would. Additionally, during Darboe's speech, whenever he made interesting points, frequently he didn't pause for applause. Perhaps he should have worked with toastmasters or public speaking coaches.

On Thursday 25th January 2007, the national assembly election as usual followed the presidential one. After the election, the APRC members in the assembly came under massive pressure from the electorate to impeach Jammeh from office due to his lavish frequent Kanilai parties and his endless extravagant gifts to foreign musicians. Jammeh's next move sent shock waves around the world. Out of the blue Jammeh declared the mighty miracle of the 21st century. He claimed to have medicine which could cure almost every available disease on the face of the planet (except cancer), diseases like HIV AIDS, asthma, diabetes, hypertension, infertility problems and many more. Perhaps it was a timely gift from God to him. That declaration brought thousands of desperate Gambians from all walks of life to seek the presidential blessing. This continued for ten more years.

In the matter of treatment, Jammeh was very strict; he wouldn't allow doctors in regular hospitals and clinics to use his medicine, and he warned against testing his medicine in laboratories.

During his tenure, a special day in the Gambian calendar was dedicated to mark the celebration of the day which Jammeh declared he'd found the cure to the aforementioned illnesses. Jammeh was now not only a head of state, but he was also a medical doctor who is willing to cure his subjects free of charge.

In order to compensate Jammeh for his kind gesture; the naive members of the national assembly would once again push their luck and test the patience of the Gambian electorate. Gradually; from late 2007 to 2010, there was conspiracy among them to promote Jammeh as the King, for a Kingdom of the Gambia. Rumours of Jammeh's Kingship became the topic of the cities, towns and rural villages. It was apparent HE would be the King of Gambia soon. However, thanks to the timely intervention of Arab revolutions across Middle East which eventually topple the leaders of Tunis, Egypt, Libya and Yemen and started Syrian civil war, he abandoned the Kingship ambition. He was worried Gambians would stage a similar uprising against him. Guess what; without a struggle with the public, in the mid 2010 NAMs quietly abandoned the fantasy of Jammeh's Kingship which they previously pledged to him.

At this time, in Jammeh's golden age, you might say, he was a revered figure in the Gambia. A handshake with him was equal to kissing a holy relic. Wherever he went, from his presidential motorcade, he would throw treats for children and bystanders who fought against each other in order to grab one.

On Thursday 24th November 2011, His Excellency Sheik Professor Dr. Alahaji Yahya AJJ Jammeh Babili Mansa Nazeru Deen completely demolished the Gambian opposition at the polls. He decisively won the election without even campaigning for it. According to him, "politics is a dirty game" and he will never compete with people whom he describes as "cockroaches and dogs". According to Jammeh, if the Gambians didn't vote for him, Jinx would vote for him. He only made a nationwide tour due to pressure from his mother Asumbi Bojang, who instructed him during the presidential campaign to travel the country and thank people for their relentless support and loyalty to him. To Jammeh, that was not a campaign. Despite all that "counterproductive behaviour", he comfortably won nearly 100% of the popular vote. From now on; Jammeh would use all his wealth of intellect as well as the resources from the might of his presidency to stave off the opposition of the people, which would slowly but surely remove him from power.

Would you be surprised if I told you Jammeh became a husband again; wife number three was Halimatu Sallah. Despite his own warning to polygamous husbands not to neglect their other wives, a few months after their wedding became public, Halimatu completely disappeared. Since then, the issue surrounding their relationship is a million dollar question which remains unanswered, and the gossip in the town continues.

In 2009 and 2010 respectively; President Jammeh gave instructions to his henchmen to round up and arrested so-called witches, and those whom he suspected to have been involved in witchcraft, across Kombou and Foni. Victims of these appalling crimes were forced to drink a mysterious liquid which intoxicated them to confess their alleged involvement in witchcraft. There was international outcry from human rights groups within the country and in the African sub-Saharan region in condemning such barbaric action.

The dramatic event of the 21st century which eventually removed Jammeh from power began shortly after the 2012 national assembly election, which was held on Thursday 29th March. In meeting with Banjul Muslims elders to mark the celebration of Muslim Eid, President Jammeh vowed to eliminate all death row inmates. Subsequently later in the same year, nine death row prisoners were executed. The move prompted four long years of diplomatic dispute between the EU and the Gambia. Consequently Jammeh further isolated Gambia from the international community.

Note: did you know that 75% of all presidential directives, directives from the office of the president and uses of executive power made in the Gambia, occurred from 2012 to 2017. President Jammeh used more executive power than any other president in the whole of Africa, except for Gaddafi in Libya. It's almost equal to President Obama's authorisation of using drones against terrorist targets. It's impossible to list the impact of all presidential directives made in the Gambia. However, the following are the most shocking moments:

The Republic of the Gambia withdrawing from the Commonwealth, the International Criminal Court, female genital mutilation, giving arresting powers to Gambia supreme Islamic council, Gambia being declared an Islamic state, the release of more than 170 prisoners, changing the Gambian electoral laws, changes of the official working hours, rice importation banned, and the declaration of Friday every week as a public holiday in the Gambia.

Under normal circumstances each of the above should be drafted in a white paper and then be proceed to the national assembly for debate as well as a vote for approval before it is implemented, as stated by the constitution. However, the office of the president did not respect the usual protocols in the Gambia. This pathetic move exacerbated public anger towards Jammeh's government. No one knows for sure the logic behind these moves; perhaps for Jammeh, it was a self-fulfilling prophecy; however, whether the public like it or not, it happened, and they had to accept it.

When I forensically examined the consciousness of Gambians, in order to resolve exactly why Jammeh lost the 2016 elections, I came to the following four conclusions.

1. It was a big mistake for Jammeh to accept the Gambian supreme Islamic council's declaration on the moon sighting saga, which forced Muslims in the Gambia to follow the Kingdom of Saudi Arabia on moon sighting, including their desire to impose the beginning and the end of the holy month of Ramadan on Muslims in the Gambia, as well as forcing Gambian Muslims to celebrate the Eid in one day. This unprecedented act greatly compromised Jammeh's relationship with the majority of Muslims across the country. This was made worse in 2014 when the security forces arrested those who refused to follow the orders from the Islamic Council. This triggered the majority of Muslims to withdraw their support.

2. The presidential executive order which declared the republic of the Gambia an Islamic state. You can imagine a secular state suddenly becoming an Islamic state frightened the minority Christian community in the country. They felt there was an urgent need to change the government in the Gambia; in my opinion, they were scared by the brutality of ISIS in the Middle East. Only a madman would ignore those concerns.

3. In the spring of 2016, while President Jammeh was on the nationwide annual Meet the People tour, he made certain unpleasant remarks against the Mandinka tribes who have a large presence in the Gambia, including a statement he made while swearing on the holy Quran that "Mandinka will never occupy the office of presidency again". It marked the beginning of Jammeh's political suicide mission. The majority of Mandinka in the sub region were baffled by that remark.

We still struggle to understand why a political leader with great responsibilities would utter such provocative remarks and create a public outcry. Cat and mouse games? A "catch me if you can" between Jammeh and Mandinka? That would not be very sensible. In the 2016 presidential election, in solidarity with the other Gambian voters, Mandinka took Jammeh to the cleaners and stripped him of all his seven titles.

4. On 16th April 2016, the leader of the main opposition party in the Gambia, lawyer Darboe was arrested, along with scores of his party executive members, for merely demonstrating to demand the release of his party supporters, who had been arrested a few days earlier on the grounds that they 'protested to demand electoral reforms without obtaining a police permit'. That added salt to the wound, particularly when it emerged that a UDP supporter called Solo Sandeng died while in the custody of the security forces. This incident would later compel opposition political parties in the Gambia to form a coalition against Jammeh.

Perhaps you may argue that President Jammeh foresaw his fall from the top. Probably at some point in 2015, he had a nightmare which shows him the end of his tenure was getting closer. Without any rational thinking, on the 20th July 2015, he suddenly bullied the IEC into changing all the relevant election rules including a one million percent increase of all electoral processing fees. In addition:

The required deposit for a presidential candidate increased from D50,000 to D500,000.

To register a new political party in the Gambia (which used to be D500) was now a whopping D1 million.

The required amount of voter card holders to endorse the registration of new political party (which used to be 500 voters) was now no less than 10,000 voters.

The deposit required for each member of national assembly to contest the election was D5000 but now that increased to a mighty D50,000.

The deposit required for a mayoral candidate used to be D2500, however suddenly it was D10,000.

The deposit required for each council candidate (which was D1250) was pushed to D5000.

Putting this in place with immediate effect consolidated Jammeh's position and cemented his grip on power. He thought it would be next to impossible for poor opposition parties to afford to contest the election. Prior to all this, way back on the 16th August 1996, when the then military captain Yahya Jammeh declared his intention to run for the presidency, he swore to the whole nation that he would not do something like this in the future.

Interestingly, since the 1996 general election, all the elections in the Gambia were held only on Thursday. The detail behind this is that when Jammeh and his mates first attempted to overthrow President Jawara's government, initially they were supposed to launch the coup on Thursday 21st July 1994. However, for some mysterious reason they faced some difficulties at Banjul international airport. They decided to wait overnight and the next day they continued their journey and the coup was a success. These were two lucky days for Jammeh and his friends.

Now, in the spirit of truth and reconciliation in the Gambia; before we complete reading this chapter, relax, get some tea or coffee, don't close the book, let's read on and collectively do some justice to Jammeh and his disciples for the benefit of our grandchildren and great-great grandchildren to come.

The developments undertaken by Jammeh's government

I don't want associate myself with those who promote vengeance against our former leaders. Our children should not grow up in an environment where hating our former leaders would be the culture and then a few decades down the line we worship them again as if they are in power. Such a trend is slowly emerging in the Gambia; to illustrate this, I can still remember very clearly back in 1994, President Jawara and his friends used to be the criminals of the day. Wherever you mentioned Jawara or his ministers, people booed them and insulted them. In addition the Gambian public were very aggressive to their families and loved ones thanks to the 'success' of the Jammeh regime. However, today, Jawara and his former ministers are the heroes of the new Gambia, thanks to the 'failure' of Jammeh and his ministers. I wonder if we are going to worship Jammeh in the future and boo President Adama Barrow as soon as he leaves office. If not, we must to learn from repeating past mistakes, and ensure that we refrain from mistreatment of our former leaders and ministers.

There is no point in preventing a child from asking silly questions. Children are curious creatures; they want to find out things, and you and I used to do exactly the same thing. Do you remember the days when you kept on asking silly questions of your grandma? Why are human beings not allowed to see God? Why is Jawara's face on all the Gambian money? Who pays President Jawara's salary? When I was a child, I would constantly bombard my grandma with questions like these.

Now let's play a little drama, without sounding like the "action man" Bala Garba Jahumpa. You can assume the role of grandpa and I will assume the role of the silly grandchild who is desperate to pass the primary school history test.

If you are ready to drink your tea, let's start the conversation with grandpa:

"Grandpa, who built the new terminal building at Banjul International airport Yundum?"

"It was built by chairman Jammeh."

"Grandpa, who constructed the bridge at Kerewan Town in NBR?"

"It was chairman Jammeh, that is why they called him Babili Mansa."

"Grandpa, who built the University of the Gambia, as well as GRTS TV?"

"It was Yaya AJJ Jammeh."

"Grandpa, who introduced the free education system in the Gambia?"

"Jammeh Musa."

"Grandpa, who built the major health centres in Farafenni, Jarra Soma, Serrekunda, Bwiam and elsewhere in the country?"

"Professor Jammeh."

"Grandpa, who undertook major road construction across the country including the coastal road?"

"Grandson, it was Dr. Yahya AJJ Jammeh."

"Grandpa, who introduced mobile phone networks and the internet in the Gambia?"

"It was Sheik Yahya Jammeh."

"Grandpa, who built dozens of high schools, middle schools and primary schools across the country?"

"His Excellency President Jammeh."

"Grandpa, who extended electricity to rural areas in the Gambia?"

"President Jammeh."

"Grandpa, who sent 77 pilgrims from the Gambia to take part in Hajji in the holy city of Mecca every year?"

"It was Captain Jammeh"

"Grandpa, who gave free scholarships to Gambians students to study abroad?"

"Mr. Jammeh, okay?"

"Grandpa, I can sense you are now getting tired. Am I boring you? Do I also sound like Bala Garba Jahumpa? One final question! Grandpa, who is the champion famer in the Gambia?"

"His Excellency Sheik Professor Dr, Alahaji Yahya AJJ Jammeh Babili Masan"

"Grandpa, I forgot to ask one ridiculous question, can I ask one more? Who gave instructions to President Adama Barrow to take his two wives wherever he goes?"

"It was Barrow's predecessor His Excellency President Yahya Jammeh Musa. Grandson, Jammeh warned polygamous husbands against neglecting their first wives otherwise he would severely punish them!"

"Wow, that is wonderful grandpa, isn't it? Grandpa, with all his achievements at hand, why do you still call Jammeh a criminal? Is such an attitude not disgusting, grandpa?"

"Grandson, let me explain. He is a pathetic dictator who is accused of thousands of human rights abuses, including murder and torture, and he forces Gambian citizens to work like slaves in his farms nationwide."

"Grandpa, I don't care about all that. It's rubbish, I would rather follow the old fashioned English concept "seeing is believing". I believed in what I saw in the infrastructure development as well as human development."

"Oh well, I can say no more to convince you. Thanks, grandson."

"Cheers, grandpa!"

In this conversation with grandpa, you can sense the behaviour of innocent children in having conversation with adults. If I use myself as example, I have never witnessed the appalling crimes of transatlantic slavery or European colonization. However, by looking at evidence from the past such as the old buildings like the Gambia High School, the Royal Victoria hospital in Banjul, as well as the slave handcuffs in the national museum etc; I know it has occurred at some point in history.

In order for children to verify the stories from the past; they must be exposed to the reality of what they can see or feel.

The records of Jammeh's appalling human rights abuse will exist in our memories for decades to come. Equally, the efforts of his nationwide infrastructure development projects will remain for centuries to come. We cannot be biased about that.

My opinion of the Gambia Truth and Reconciliation Commission

I applauded lawyer Ousainou Darboe for his decision to forgive Jammeh and his government for all the pain they inflicted on him. When I read Darboe's forgiveness in the newspaper he instantly earned my respect. For him to forgive the former president for what his government did to Darboe and his party is unprecedented. Can you imagine; a man who was unlawfully detained and subsequently sent to prison for three years, of which he served at least nine months. From the business perspective alone, during his detention lawyer Darboe lost many clients, including many of his political party supporters. The essence of being a Politician mean every day spent in jail means a loss of credibility as well as party support. As a result the UDP party nearly disappeared from the Gambian political map. Despite all that Darboe swallowed his pride and forgave; that was fantastic. For me, Gambia's reconciliation started from there.

As I have said, to be honest with you, I am not any fan of revenge; neither am I a supporter of vengeance especially against our former rulers. I don't mind if you disagree with me. The beauty of democracy is having the chance to maturely debate burning issues. After all, if you let me explain my points, we might be agreeing on principle.

The foundation for my argument is based on the following questions. Why do citizens of Africa desire so much to send our former leaders into exile until they rot in anguish? Why could we not, as free citizens of the world, effectively dealt with them with a European style of democracy and resolve the burning issues which turn them in to monsters before it's too late? Each African country should strive to install effective institutions like an independent judiciary system, and strong legislative bodies which would hold executives accountable without hindrance. The threat of prison and exile for African leaders has failed to deter them from committing crimes while in office.

Most European countries abolished the death penalty because to them it no longer deters people from committing heinous crimes like murder. In the Gambia, Jammeh froze Jawara and his minsters' assets and their properties, but Jammeh wasn't prevented from accumulating his own assets and valuable property. The fundamental problems which cause leaders to become dictators, tyrants and authoritarians - including the concept of the divine right of kings and public lack of political awareness - are still prevalent in our societies.

You will be shocked when you read later on how many African leaders have been sent to prison, assassinated or sent to exile (there is a list at the end of this chapter). The number is sky-rocketing. Don't tell me "Yaya, you are not the victim of any of their crimes, and you sound like a priest in the church". Of course I am a victim; let me tell you my own story which happened during the 2016 Gambia political impasses.

Someone, I guess a Jammeh thug, called me in the middle of the night using a withheld number and told me to stop writing in Facebook: unless I began to write something positive about Jammeh and his government, he threatened to sort me out. Guess what? I refused to follow his orders. Thanks God it's all over now otherwise this book might not have been published.

We cannot build the Gambia and attain economic super power status in Africa if we fail to learn how to forgive one another.

My recommendation for the new Gambian government

I think President Barrow's government should establish a Commission for Compensation. This humanitarian scheme could be established alongside the incoming Truth and

Reconciliation commission. The purpose of this commission will be to give financial assistance to families of victims who die under unlawful detention. Additionally, the commission could lend supporting hands to those who suffered physical torture inflicted by the past regime. The criteria must be set for each crime committed which would warrant any form of compensation. There must be clear guidelines to ensure the smooth running of commissions. And the general public must be strictly encouraged to follow the rules and guidelines as stated by the commission.

For any case to warrant compensation, it should have happened within the period from 1996 to the end of 2016; the period stated by the current Reconciliation commission. The commission would look at each and every single claim and subsequently consider genuine claims. The amount of cash should be allocated to each family victim accordingly. To support this initiative, the government of the Gambia could create a special fundraising scheme which will target private citizens as well as individual businesses, NGO's and foreign aid to seek donations. In my opinion this measure would be more effective rather than pursuing the former president and his officials to stand trial and send them to jail for alleged crimes they have committed.

We should note that Africa and the Middle East are breeding grounds for dictatorship based on the hereditary system, while the aristocratic system is common in Europe. Apart from hanging Nazi leaders and their allies in late 1940s and 1950s, Europeans, Americans and Australians do not send their ex-leaders to prison, exile them, or assassinate them. Let us recently use the examples of US president George W. Bush, former British Prime Minister Tony Blair and Silvio Berlusconi, the former Italian Prime Minister.

In 2003, Bush and Blair illegally invaded Iraq; as result thousands of their countrymen and women perished in the struggle, along with hundreds of thousands of Iraqis. Billions of pounds sterling were spent to sponsor the war. However neither Bush nor Blair ever stood trial to face justice. Their country's strong institution successfully defended them and subsequently blamed the crimes on the poor intelligence failure. In the UK, the government established the commission of inquiry led by a reputable judge called Lord Chilcot. After spending millions of pounds as well as thousands of hours of manpower, at the end of their investigation, they reached the conclusion which set Tony Blair free and pointed the finger at poor intelligent service. Amazingly, the US government doesn't even recognise the finding of this commission of inquiry.

The former Italian Prime Minister Silvio Berlusconi has faced hundreds of allegations ranging from corruption to having sex with a minor. However he never served a single night in a cell for any of those crimes committed. He is presently cleared of any crime.

Why won't Africans wake from their long sleep? Why does Africa systematically fail to learn from these examples? We must establish a strong institution which would serve the citizens and protect the leaders from future humiliation.

I understand the public's frustration and anger towards Jammeh and his government because of the terrible social and economic crimes they may have committed in the country. This included allegations of murder, torture and abduction, and the country is horribly divided. I really feel sorry for all the victims. And they must understand that we are all equal in this. That said, what will Gambia gain by sending former government officials to jail? It may well cause some social problems due to the following factors:

All those Muslims sent to Mecca by president Jammeh to perform Hajji.

Schools build to educate Gambian children.

Hospitals built to provide healthcare for Gambian families.

Free education for Gambian children.

Citizens of the Gambia who received medals for their service for the country.

All this might became irrelevant to society if Jammeh was ever convicted of any crime and sent to prison. Psychological trauma and shame will be huge for the beneficiaries of Jammeh. Those who perform hajji may feel betrayed by the system as well as disgrace in relation to their religious obligations. Patients receiving treatment from their hospital beds would feel awkward bearing in mind a convicted criminal provided it for them. Students learning from class rooms provided by him would feel ashamed by the fact that the school was built by a criminal. Servicemen and women, civil servants and civil society who received medals from him would feel disgusted and cheated of their services to the country.

The impact would be similar to Olympic athletes who won double gold medals and later on the medals are stripped from them due to drug enhancement in achieving that victory; can you imagine the horror for the athlete's fans and the betrayal they will feel for being cheated of their moment of celebration?

You can equally argue that the money and the resources spent to achieve those things have come from the state coffers and that is the truth; however in the Gambian psychology Jammeh is accredited with all that.

This book serves my truth and reconciliation. I think from the best of my ability I stated all the facts available to me without fear or favour. The number one audience I will target to read the book is President Jammeh himself, his former government officials and Gambian political elites. APRC members may feel I have been critical of them and might be disappointed with me for that; however there is nothing better than to learn from past mistakes and ensure you never repeat them again, then move on with your life and look forward to the future.

Here is one more example from the time of the prophet Muhammad while in Mecca. The holy Quran has been critical on some individuals and their families; however it didn't prevent them from reading it and later on they even became Muslims. Amazingly none of them ever attempted to delete those verses from the holy Quran. As a civilised society we must help each other to state the facts when they are available; that is really essential to unity as well as building the nation; this fact may be critical for you today and equally it could be critical on me tomorrow.

Jammeh's relationship with Marabouts and fortune tellers

There is a distinction between Marabouts and fortune tellers. Marabouts are the ancient psychological doctors. Their service to society is still very relevant; this includes providing spiritual counselling, religious advice, and offering prayers for people. They give hope and provide a comfortable environment for societies, and use diplomatic skills during time of crisis to solve disputes within communities. Their service is vital in social ceremonies such as weddings, naming ceremonies, funerals and other important religious gatherings.

Fortune tellers are individuals who usually perform various ritualistic predictions of the past, present and future. Frequently they perform traditional healing such as exorcism and faith healing. The resources they use for their service usually come from the forest and the natural world: tree roots, leaves and suchlike. Traditionally, there is huge demand for their services and they remain a very important symbol of African culture. However there are a minority among them who claim to have miraculous powers and abilities to communicate with spirits, angles, jinx and devils. Such claims create controversy.

President Jammeh, like many people in society, ridiculed them in the public but worshipped them in secret. However a minority of them are unscrupulous individuals. Excessive use of their services could easily lead someone to overestimate their abilities. Perhaps something like that led Jammeh to believe that the democratic process or military coups would not remove him from power. It may also have strengthened his confidence and reinforced his belief that he would stay in power for ever (remember his most famous remark when he stated that "if God wills it, I would stay in power for one billion years"- unfortunately for Jammeh it only lasted for 22 years and six months). It might also have exacerbated the large numbers of animal sacrifices he undertook. Or perhaps you might say he was being generous to the poor and needy.

Note: animal sacrifice is a very important part of the Muslims religion. Two thirds of all animal sacrifices worldwide for religious purposes are done in Muslim countries. It's an essential part of our religion.

The ritual practises of Marabouts and fortune tellers are widespread around the world. Different communities use their services in the different ways. Overall, with the increase scientific discoveries, public demand on their services is gradually declining. However, in Africa that is not the case. They still actively sustain their role in society (thus there are few clinical psychological doctors in Africa, for example, because of this).

Jammeh versus Ecowas - 42 days of political standoff

In November 2016, the IEC welcomed all political parties in the Gambia to submit their nomination certificates to the IEC headquarters, situated at Bertil Harding Highway, Kanifing. Under Gambia's constitution, each political party is required to submit all necessary documents before they can contest the election as presidential candidates.

Three candidates - Yahya Jammeh, Adama Barrow and Mamma Kandeh - all submitted their documents as required and all were subsequently nominated for the election which was scheduled to take place on Thursday 1st December 2016. The campaign lasted just two weeks. Apart from 2001 election, this was one of the most contested elections Gambia ever witnessed. The campaign was trouble-free and according to most observers, the election was free and fair. All three candidates travelled nationwide to sell themselves, their ideas and their vision to the people. On Thursday 1st December,

Gambians went to poll to cast their vote to choose the next leader of the country.

The following day around noon, the final result was announced and Mr Adama Barrow, the coalition candidate was declared the winner. Initially the country went wild with exuberance. The nation's euphoria in celebrating the unthinkable was unprecedented. On that day I made the following remarks, published in the Daily Observer newspaper:

"I am a firm believer that a divine power is always revealed when people are genuinely praying for it, especially during a time of need. As someone who comes from a Marabout family background; from my childhood I got used to one phrase which is "Peace is prevailed in the Gambia because she has been protected by the prayers of our ancestor". This Marabout phrase has become reality again. On the 2nd December 2016 President Jammeh conceded defeat shortly after the IEC chairman's declaration of the election results. This unprecedented move has created euphoria a kind of which I never witnessed in the history of the Gambia. After the result was announced, I went out to see people's mood. I saw many tens of thousands of peoples celebrating in the street at every corner of Banjul and Serrekunda Westfield junction all the way to Brikama; everyone was joyfully celebrating the victory of the coalition candidate Mr. Adama Barrow. For the first time in 22 years, I saw Gambians at every level freely expressing themselves in all manners. And I was no exception; I joined with the crowd to celebrate as I did back in 1994.

It's exactly why I find it difficult to resist the temptation not to share my own unique euphoria with readers. I remember back in July 22nd 1994 when president Jammeh came to power, as a 29 year old young soldier I felt the same euphoria at that time as well. However this time is different because I know the true meaning of what regime changes means.

My message to fellow Gambians is as follows:

Can we kindly join together as one Gambia and massively thank the IEC chairman Alieu Momar Njai for playing this crucial role which ensures the election was free and fair. I think he proved to be right when he stated "our election is second to none in the world". Additionally in this mood of celebration let us whole heartily commend his Excellency the

President of republic of the Gambia Dr. Yahya AJJ Jammeh for accepting the election result. Can we also thank him for serving our wonderful nation for 22 years; with all controversy; I think it's worth remembering him as a man who loves this country at heart, and he made many tremendous development efforts in infrastructure, making education accessible for all, improving the health sector and promoting agriculture. However, as human beings we are not perfect: ruling a country for 22 year cannot be possible without the country and its rulers facing many challenges; but as we celebrate this glorious victory let's remember the positive aspects of Jammeh and his regime.

Finally; am sending my warmest congratulations to the President Elect his Excellency Mr Adama Barrow, his entire team and coalition partners for this glorious victory. May God bless you all and give you strength in all your endeavours wherever is possible in order to enable you to lead our beloved country peacefully.

My advice to every Gambian is that now the election is over, let's put aside our political difference and come together as one Gambia, one people. The country is belonging to all of u. Let's maintain peace, stability, brotherhood, and preserve the country's peace not just for ourselves but for our future generations as well."

On Thursday 8th December it was announced over GRTS that President Jammeh would address the nation on the following day. On Friday 9th December 2016 in the 10 o'clock news headlines, the GRTS newscaster dropped the bombshell from President Jammeh which later became known as the Gambian political impasse. Later the same day, Jammeh appeared on TV and angrily told the jubilant nation that he rejected the election result entirely. I will never forget that moment of horror he inflicted on us that day. 42 days of grief started from there. I can still remember the horror on the newsreader's face as he read the full statement live on GRTS (the full story, including the statement from Jammeh and the coalition which followed, is included in Chapter Six of this book).

On Tuesday 13th December, a delegation comprising three heads of state from Liberia (Ellen Johnson Sirleaf), Ghana

(John Mahama), and Nigeria (Muhammadu Buhari) arrived in the Gambia to mediate the political impasse. This team became known as the Ecowas fact finding mission to Gambia, and was led by the Liberian president. They made similar trips back and forth to resolve the impasse without any luck. On their final mediation trip to Banjul, on Friday 13th January 2017, the team took Adama Barrow into hiding while they threatened Jammeh with military action to eventually force him to exile and install Barrow in his rightful position.

On 12th December, the APRC filed a petition to the Gambia Supreme Court in Banjul to demand the court declare the election result null and void and require a new election. Eventually the Supreme Court did not proceed with the case due to a lack of judges to see the petition. However we can borrow some court proceedings moments and determine our own conclusion from there. I would assume the position of Jammeh and the APRC, while you can assume the role of the judge.

Jammeh and the APRC:

"My lord, I request you to null and void the results of 2016 election on the ground of the following reasons:

1: The day after the election the opposition supporters insulted me and insulted my mother, some even went to the length to announce the death of my beloved mother on social media as well as harassing and intimidating my APRC supporters in the country.

2: 360919 vote card holders nationwide did not cast their vote. Why?

3: My lord, on the 2nd December 2016 the IEC declared Mr Adama Barrow the winner of the election. The total amount of registered voters in the Gambia is 886578 voters. Mr Adama Barrow received 263515 votes, Yahya Jammeh received 212099 votes and Mamma Kandeh received 102969 votes. The majority of Barrow was 51416. However, my lord, on 5th December 2016, the same IEC subsequently changed their mind and announced the second result. Which indicated the following: the total amount of people who voted for Adama Barrow is 227708, Yahya Jammeh had 208487 votes and Mamma Kandeh 89768 votes. This time Barrow's majority is 19224. My lord, how come there was one election and two different results declared by the IEC?

4: My lord, over 5000 APRC supporters in URR were not allow to vote by the IEC due to irregularities in the voters card registration system, and they were later told to return home because the election was already won by the Coalition.

5: My lord, in 2011 and 2016 respectively, Ecowas refused to send election observers to the Gambia, because they claimed the election was not going to be free and fair. My lord, how can Ecowas now act as mediators of our political impasse?

6: My lord, it is stated in the constitution that anyone can challenge the election result at court within ten days' time; however, if the outcome of the court decision is not relevant to the election result and stops the inauguration from taking place then why is this stated in the constitution and giving the chance to losers to challenge the result at court?

The judge:

"Mr President, thank you for your election petition. It's a pleasure to hear your case. Unfortunately, there are not enough judges in the court to constitute the panel you deserve to look at your petition.

However, I will answer all your queries at once:

1: We are in the 21st century: when you occupied public office, you have handed over your private life to the world.

2: Mr President, in a democratic process all the registered voters do not always participate in the election. Don't you remember in the recent US election, nearly 95 million registered voters didn't cast their vote; in the United Kingdom in 2015, nearly 8 million registered voters didn't cast their vote either.

3: Mr President, your representatives were all present while the entire vote was counted and they accepted the outcome of the vote. I cannot help you with that.

4: Mr President how did you able to read the mind of 5000 peoples to determine they were going to vote for you? Whether they are APRC supporters or not, people change their mind at the ballot box.

5: Mr President, according to Ecowas' charter, Ecowas is mandated to intervene and resolve the dispute even if they refused to observe past elections.

6: Mr President, the constitution mandated the IEC to conduct the election and declare the winner. And according to the constitution the declared winner would have to assume the office when your mandate ends. Mr President I would recommend for you to step down at the end of your mandate.

What is interesting is in the election petition Jammeh has some valid points. One is this; how come Ecowas intervened now when they had clearly stated in previous years there was not going to be a free and fair election and refused to observe two previous elections in the Gambia? Were they no longer 'friends' with Jammeh and as a result they wanted him out at any cost?

Also, the constitution is not clear about election petitions. What is the point of allowing someone to file a petition to court if the outcome of that court proceeding is not relevant to the case?

All that the IEC stated in their press release was that there was an error while they tabled the results. However, they never indicated whether it was due to computer error or a typing error.

Perhaps President Jammeh was not a very good debater. That is why the more he appeared on national TV to argue his election fraud case; the more he dug himself into a hole. In the speeches he made on GRTS about the 2016 political impasse, it sounded like he was expressing frustration and anger at his loss, rather than being aggressive towards Gambians. I had confidence that there would be no military conflict. On that occasion he was more diplomatic than usual. His initial acceptance of the result had totally discredited the credibility of his later argument, despite some valid points which consolidate his position.

Hopefully with our newly found freedom, people will be able to express themselves more freely. I can still vividly remember the election night in 2016. The programme presenters on national TV were so scared to express their own opinion. When it appeared that President Jammeh was losing the election, all that they could blame was voter apathy. I am sure in future elections we will be able to express our opinion freely, like Europe and America does.

Note: Here is a list of the African leaders of the past 60 years who have been sent to exile, assassinated or executed while in power or shortly after leaving office:

1. Laurent Desire Kabila - DRC Congo - assassinated

2. Mabutu Sese Seko - DRC Congo - exile

3. Patrice Lumumba - DRC Congo - assassinated

4. Jean Bedel Bokassa - Central African Republic - exile

5. Ahned Al-Mirghani - Sudan - exile

6. Thomas Sankara - Burkina Faso - assassinated

7. Blaise Compaore - Burkina Faso - exile

8. Joao Bernardo Vieira - Guinea Bissau - exile and later assassinated

9. Moussa Daddy Camara - Guinea Conakry - exile

10. Jerry Rawlings - Ghana - exile

11. Sani Abacha - Nigeria - assassinated

12. Murtala Mohammad - Nigeria - assassinated

13. Omar Al-Bashir - Sudan - ICC indicted

14. Amadou Toumani Toure - Mali - exile

15. Laurent Gbagbo -Ivory Coast - ICC indicted, currently on trial

16. Charles Taylor - Liberia - exile, currently serving jail

17. Samuel Doe - Liberia - assassinated

18. Muammar Gaddafi - Libya - assassinated

19. Anwar Sadat - Egypt - assassinated

20. Hosni Mubarak - Egypt - currently in detention

21. Zine El Abidine Ben Ali - Tunisia - exile

22. Idi Amin - Uganda - died in exile

23. Haile Mariam - Ethiopia executed

24. Haile Selassie - Ethiopia - assassinated

25. Siad Barre - Somalia - died in exile

26. Juvenal Habyarimana - Rwanda - assassinated in plane crash

27. Cyprien Ntary Amira - Burundi - assassinated in plane crash

28. Hissene Habre - Chad - currently on trial

29. Yahya Jammeh - Gambia - exile

30. Dawda Jawara - Gambia - exile and now returned home.

31. Kwame Nkrumah - Ghana – exile

CHAPTER 5
THE IEC DROPPED A BOMBSHELL WHICH NEARLY SET GAMBIA ON FIRE

Friday morning after election night; shortly before lunch time, the chairman of the Independent Electoral Commission, Alieu Momar Njai, announced the final result and declared Mr Adama Barrow the winner of the 2016 presidential election. Momentarily, with euphoria, I didn't know whether to laugh louder or to cry and squeeze out all my tears.

The following Monday, 5th December 2016, the same IEC dropped the bombshell which ignited the fire of political battle and put Jammeh on a collision course with Ecowas. It was a period of a Machiavellian style of politics.

If we ask ourselves why the coalition won the 2016 election, there is no doubt: President Jammeh massively contributed to his own downfall. You may recall, since the 2011 presidential election, Jammeh had run out of economic and political steam. As a result his political rhetoric was increasingly designed to marginalising Gambians at every level without their knowledge. In 2012 during his meeting with Banjul elders he threatened to kill death row inmates (nine were executed in Mile 2 central prison). In the following years he gave more ammunition to his opponents by declaring Gambia an Islamic state which compromised minority Christians, threatened to exterminate Mandinka tribes if they crossed the line, and gave power to the Gambia Supreme Islamic Council to arrest those who wouldn't follow their orders on moon sightings (more on this in Chapter Six).

An aside: here's what I wrote when Jammeh declared Gambia an Islamic state:

"The Gambia has become latest country in Africa to be declared an Islamic republic. Most countries in West Africa have large Muslim populations. However, few have ever been declared an Islamic republic. Of a population of nearly two million people, almost 85% of which are

Muslims, and such declaration is welcomed by majority of Muslims in the Gambia. As a Muslim, there is always a desire and ambition to fully adhere to Islamic values and principles, abide by its rules, laws and live by its example. If such declaration is properly implemented, it might help the country to grow intellectually, which may result in more jobs and small businesses, more religious tolerance, and increase people's awareness of Islamic values and decrease anti- social behaviour such as tribalism. However, in today's world Islamic countries and Muslims around the world are facing many different challenges. Gambia is not immune to these, for example:

(1) maintaining law and order to ensure there are no self-appointed clerics to enforce Islamic rules and values on everyone.

(2) to ensure the Christian minority and non-Muslims are not marginalised or face any form of prejudice in the country.

(3) to ensure fake Jihads Sheiks from Middle East would not be able to introduce any form of religious violence, radical views, extreme ideologies and cause hatred between Muslims and non-Muslims.

(4) to ensure the ownership of land and property is properly implemented to the best interest of citizens in order to discourage millionaires and billionaires from the Middle East acquiring the land.

All this is to ensure safety and guarantee protection for all citizens from becoming hostages and slaves in their own country, like what is happing in Mauritania, Northern Mali, Niger, Sudan, and many other part of North Africa; It must be a moral obligation for the international community to fight against such practises."

On the other hand, Mr Adama Barrow is the luckiest man in 21st century political history, not only in the Gambia, but throughout the world. Shortly after he assumed the leadership role of the UDP party, I read his biography in the newspapers. To me, there were many striking similarities with the former UK Conservative leader from 2001 to 2003, Mr Ian Duncan-Smith; a quiet caretaker, who was waiting in limbo and would be soon be pushed to the side. Adama Barrow was lucky, like the British Prime Minister from 2010 to 2016, David Cameron, a political newcomer who was relatively unknown. In 2005, Cameron successfully became the leader of the UK Conservative party and after the 2010 UK general election, he took the advantage of the hung parliament to form a coalition government with the UK Liberal Democrat party and became the Prime Minister, as well as relegating his former boss William Hague, the Conservative leader from 1997 to 2001, to the role of UK Foreign Secretary. It was exactly the same political scenario for Adama Barrow; the coalition of seven different political parties brought him a decisive win and he relegated his former boss lawyer Ousainou Darboe, the leader of UDP from 1996 to 2016, to fill the role of Gambia's Foreign Minister.

I'm wondering if President Barrow will try his luck like David Cameron, and contest the next general election to rule the Gambia with his own mandate. Or will he honour the coalition agreement which is supposed to be a three year transitional term? If not, will he serve the maximum full five years constitutional term and step aside for someone else?

Finger crossed: President Adama Barrow will not use the usual political rhetoric of other African leaders, for example "My country still loves me and I want to serve them as much as I can. I have started some very important development projects and I am not going leave the office until I complete them." Such a move will put his legacy in jeopardy. Perhaps he will even risk being booed at the public gatherings similar to what we have witnessed during the 2017 Independent celebration at the Independent Stadium Bakau: following the announcement of the presence of the former vice president Ajaratu Isatou Njai Seedy, she received a massive public boo from the angry crowd.

Note: Niccolo Machiavelli, an Italian political philosopher and the founder of modern political science, who lived from 1469 to 1527, stated in his famous book *The Prince* that "the virtue of leadership is wisdom, strategy, strength, ruthlessness and niceness". However, I would like to add the following sentiment: with the prevalence of social media and the diversity of modern democracy, modern political leaders should be equipped with the modern political philosophy in order to intellectually stay in touch with wider society.

The British political philosopher Thomas Hobbes (1588 to 1679), who provoked the debates of the theory of divine right of Kings" and the theory of social contracts, made a remarkable statement in his book *Leviathan* that "men may face many evil consequences, yet the consequences of the want of it, which is perpetual war of every man against his neighbour, are much worse. Human affairs cannot be without some inconvenience." I think such an attitude caused the Gambian political crisis.

I did my best to tell the stories of the political impasse from different angles so that I can give a fair treatment to everyone involved. I fully covered the whole crisis period from 1st December 2016 to 21st January 2017. The stories are very fascinating and exciting. The intense political atmosphere in the country at that stage was equal to spending a night in a war zone. The power struggle between President Jammeh and President Elect Adama Barrow has felt like sharing a bedroom with your ex-partner's newly wedded husband.

The forty two days and three hours of the Gambian political impasse ended with President Jammeh's final address to the nation a few hours after he relinquished power on Friday 20th January 2017. The next day, Saturday 21st January 2017, he went to exile in Equatorial Guinea.

(All quotes here are from the Point newspaper, unless otherwise stated)

The final speech of President Yahya Jammeh:

"My first pre-occupation as President and commander-in-chief of the Armed Forces, and a patriot, and the most sacred at that, is to preserve at every instance and in every circumstance, the lives of Gambians.

And this is a duty, I hold sacred as I have always strive for peace and security of our nation and Africa.

During this entire time that Allah SWT in his infinite wisdom has permitted me to exercise power, and throughout the time that the sovereign people of The Gambia have put their confidence in me, my primary pre-occupation has been to uphold the dignity of our people and the sovereignty of this great nation.

As a result of all the numerous sacrifices that we and those before us have made as a nation, The Gambia has affirmed its desire to determine its own future and destiny.

This is a course I have always been ready to defend, and even with my life. All the actions we have taken towards building this nation up to this point have distinguished us among the community of nations and given us pride of place in history.

All this while, as a Muslim and a patriot, I believed it is not necessary that a single drop of blood be shed, since the beginning of this political impasse that our dear nation is going through. I promised before Allah SWT and the entire nation that all the issues we currently face will be resolved peacefully.

I am indeed thankful to Allah SWT that up till now not even a single causality has been registered. I believe in the importance of dialogue, and in the capacity of Africans to resolve among themselves all the challenges on the way towards democracy, economic and social development.

It is as a result of this that I have decided today, in good conscience, to relinquish the mantle of leadership of this country, our great nation, with infinite gratitude to all Gambians, women, children, youths and men and friends of The Gambia who have supported me for 22 years in the building of a modern Gambia.

I put above, all and everything, the independence of the free and proud people of The Gambia, and I will always together with you defend this independence that we so dearly fought and won.

My decision today was not dictated by anything else, but by the supreme interest of you the Gambian people and our dear country, taking into consideration my prayer and desire that peace and security continue to reign in The Gambia.

At a time when we are witnessing trouble and fear in other parts of Africa and the world, the peace and security of The Gambia is our collective heritage, which we must jealously guard and defend.

I am proud and honoured to have served our country The Gambia.

While thanking all of you, men, women and children, members of the armed and security services, humble citizens and all those who have supported me, and those who were against me during this period, I implore them all to put the supreme interest of our nation, The Gambia, above all partisan interest and endeavour working together as one nation, to continue to preserve the highly cherished achievements of the country's sovereignty, peace, stability and integrity, as well as the economic achievements realised during these years.

I pray that The Gambia our homeland continues to be united and prosperous for the welfare of each and every one of us, and be the pride of all.

I summit myself only to the judgement of Allah SWT whose judgement is above all and beyond man, time and history.

The Almighty Allah SWT is the only guarantor of truth and justice.

Finally, I am truly and sincerely proud to have been of service to you and our noble nation.

I wish to thank each and every one of the security forces, members of governments present and past, my party militants and most importantly you the Gambian people and National Assembly members, past and present, for the confidence vested in me and your loyal support.

I pray that Allah SWT continues to light our path and to shower his mercy and blessings on our great and beautiful country.

I wish to take this opportunity to thank my mother, my wife and children for all their prayers and support throughout the past 22 years.

I thank you all, and may Allah SWT continue to bless our motherland."

The reaction of President Elect Barrow the day after Jammeh contested the election results:

The President Elect Adama Barrow told the press on Saturday, 10 December, that the president should step down to maintain his global applauded decision he made voluntarily, a week ago and must know that he has no constitutional authority to reject the results of the election.

He recalled that on December 1, the Gambia held its presidential elections and on the 2 December, the results were declared according to law.

According to President Elect Barrow, the incumbent candidate called him to congratulate him for his victory. He said the outgoing president told him in a simple, clear language that the results were the verdict of people and God.

"The gesture was applauded both at home and abroad. The Gambia earned a respectable place in the international community and everybody applauded the action of the outgoing president. This earned the outgoing president and my humble self as incoming president a place in the Gambia and world history," said Barrow.

"Yesterday the outgoing president issued a statement on the national media to reject the results of the election. He declared it as invalid and promised to hold fresh elections. I wish to inform you that the outgoing president has no constitutional authority to reject the results of the election and order for fresh elections to be held," he said.

He clarified that IEC is the only competent authority to announce the results of election and to declare a winner, adding it has already done so and he is now the president-elect. He said President Jammeh is the outgoing president and he is to handover executive powers to him when his term expires in January.

"I wish to call on all Gambians to go about their businesses. We have impressed the world for delivering a free, fair and credible election. I am advising supporters of the coalition to celebrate the victory with discipline and prepare themselves for the inaugurations in January after the end of term of the outgoing president," he said.

He said in the interim, he has opened up a channel of communication to try to convince him to facilitate a smooth transfer of executive powers in the supreme interest of this country.

Barrow said "I told him in our telephone conversation that we were both born in 1965. We are the children of the independence and it would be an honour to have the smooth transfer of executive power for the first time in the history done by two citizens who were born in the year the Gambia became independent. I would want him to join me as president of the

Second Republic along with ex-president Jawara of the First Republic in January to commemorate the birth of the third republic when I assume office."

"Let him know that leaders come and go. Sooner or later, I must also go. This is a fact that all of us act at all times in the supreme interest of the Gambia. I urge him to change his current position and accept the verdict of the people in good faith for the sake of the Gambia our homeland whose people deserve to live in peace, freedom and prosperity," Barrow concluded.

Additionally - Mr Halifa Sallah, the spokesperson said the outgoing president called the president-elect and indicated that he was willing for a smooth transfer of power and that would require setting up two teams, one from each side and they will negotiate because running a government is about running ministries, public corporations. So it means that if you are transferring power, you are transferring the strategic plans, programmes of actions and projects, so it is important to have a transitional phase where the two teams will work together to be able to get an inventory of what is happening on the other side, he said.

He said this is to ensure that the next cabinet ministers will not face a vacuum. According to Sallah, this was working well until the outgoing president made the change of decision on Friday which upset the whole agenda. He said the IEC has been communicating to all parties and are being transparent all along.

He stated that the Constitution of the Gambia made it clear that the incoming president should assume office upon the expiration of the term of the outgoing president. He urged the Gambian people to do away with the mentality of whether Jammeh will insist but people must know that if he does that he is doing an unlawful act.

The GDC's statement on Jammeh's rejection of the election results:

Friday the 9th of December 2016, following the announcement by President Yahya Jammeh on state television that he is rejecting the election results; the leader of the Gambia Democratic Congress (GDC) Mamma Kandeh has indicated that the GDC has no plans to contest another election.

According to a text message sent to this paper by the press secretary of GDC Essa Jallow, The Gambia Democratic Congress has learnt of President Yahya Jammeh's decision to reject the 2016 election results.

"The move contravenes the Constitution of The Gambia, GDC has accepted the outcome of the elections and that our position remains unchanged. The Gambian people have elected Adama Barrow in a free, fair and transparent election which President Jammeh himself initially accepted and GDC has no plans to contest it," the GDC leader maintains.

Hon. Mamma Kandeh therefore urged President Jammeh to reverse his decision in the interest of peace and stability. "Your swift decision earlier to concede defeat and your subsequent move to call Adama Barrow to congratulate him was lauded throughout the world. We therefore prevail on you to reconsider your decision," Mamma Kandeh added.

The GDC leader Hon. Mamma Kandeh, therefore appeals to all Gambians to remain calm while the situation is being resolved.

Note: the GDC is a new political party established in the Gambia in early 2016, and led by Mamma Kandeh, a former APRC member of parliament. However the party managed to poll significant numbers of votes during the 2016 presidential elections, which is unusual in the Gambia political history. This is largely due to the matured leadership style of Mamma Kandeh as well as his popularity among women and young people particularly those living in urban areas. The party was recently rated by many political pundits as Gambia's second main opposition party, and they expect to perform well in national assembly elections and presidential elections to come.

Shortly after Jammeh left office, he delivered this short statement through the state media:

"I hereby wish President Adama Barrow all the best from the bottom of my heart. The Almighty Allah has decided, and I will be found wanting if I as a Muslim and a former president do not sincerely wish him and his administration all the best," Jammeh said.

He added: "For the welfare of all Gambians, anytime my advice and support is needed by President Adama Barrow, I am ready to offer him sincere advice and services.

"On this note, I hereby donate to President Adama Barrow all the rice that is harvested in my Vision 2016 farms. This is the entire harvest for him to give to women who have been helping at the farms in the CRR."

On 9th December 2016, President Jammeh rejected the 2016 election results:

President Jammeh has called for a fresh election, barely a week after conceding defeat to Adama Barrow in the December 1st presidential election.

He described the recently-concluded polls as one marked by 'errors and mistakes' at the level of the Independent Electoral Commission (IEC).

Jammeh made the call in a televised statement delivered on state TV on Friday night.

"This is the most dubious elections that we have ever had in this country. It is unacceptable, and we will go back to the polls. Because I want to make sure that every Gambian has voted under an Independent Electoral Commission that is independent, neutral and free from foreign influence.

"We must hold a clean, transparent election where nobody will be denied the right to vote, and where the election will be supervised by God-fearing, honest and patriotic IEC members."

He said elections are not football matches where the results are final, whether the referee is wrong or right.

"In football, whether the referee was correct or wrong, the results are final. This is election, where people decide their destiny and so if the referee is wrong, the results cannot be final.

"This being the case, we will go back to the polls; we will organize fresh elections and also make sure that everybody is registered."

He further stated: "Time will tell and Allah will judge, when we will go back to the polls. As a government, we will meet and work out and see how soon we can go back to the electorate, depending on the limited resources that we have.

"It is very expensive; this is the second time we are financing election on

our own. If we had all the resources, we will call an immediate election."

He also said the IEC was not independent, describing its work as "treacherous".

"We also have an IEC that is not independent, and so we have to make sure that the next time we have election, the treachery that happened this time would not be repeated.

"I don't want any vengeance. I will not also tolerate any demonstrations, and the security services of this country are here to maintain law and order. The peace and stability of this country cannot be compromised", he further stated.

Jammeh also warned against vengeance and violence in the country, whilst calling for peace, saying that everybody should go about their lawful business.

The above summary is from the statement made by Jammeh in his long speech on national TV. Initially Jammeh astonished the world when he first conceded election defeat, however, one week later, he did exactly what people expected of him, changed his mind and rejected the result. There are many conflicting stories as to why that happened. Some say some of his cabinet ministers led him to believe that the election was rigged by the IEC. Alternatively, there is article published in the Voice newspaper which claims that Jammeh was influenced by Robert Mugabe, the President of Zimbabwe since 1987, who brainwashed Jammeh into rejecting the election result on the ground that is "un-African" to remove political leaders by the ballot box. The same story stated Mugabe promised to reveal to Jammeh the techniques he used to stay in power when he was in a similar position back in 2008. He would support Jammeh even if it meant providing military assistance. But for some unknown reason, Mr Mugabe soon disappeared from the equation. I am sure in the near future, whatever led Jammeh to this dramatic U-turn will be revealed.

On Monday 5th December 2016, the IEC dropped the bombshell which nearly unleashed civil war in the Gambia and eventually ignited the Gambian political impasse of forty two days and three hours:

"The tabulation of the 2016 Presidential election results from fifty three constituencies was done correctly, the Independent Electoral Commission (IEC) disclosed yesterday.

In a press release sent to this paper, it also stated: "Furthermore, regional election results were also tabulated correctly from Banjul to Basse Administrative Areas. However, when the total votes per region were being tallied, certain figures were inadvertently transposed.

"Instead of adding the total number of votes polled by Adama Barrow in Basse administrative area, the IEC added the total number of ballots cast for Basse administrative area to Adama Barrow's total number of votes thus swelling the number of votes Mr Barrow polled nationally.

This error was repeated across for other contesting candidates.

Having noticed this, the error is now corrected and this is the actual result:

Barrow Adama 227, 708 votes

Jammeh, Yahya AJJ Sheikh Prof. Alh. Dr 208, 487 votes

Kandeh Mamma 89, 768 votes

This result which has not changed the status quo was unanimously endorsed by the representatives of the contesting candidates at the Election House" yesterday morning 5th December 2016

Barrow 43%, Jammeh 40% and Kandeh 17%"

Note: after I heard the above press release from the IEC on the GRTS 6 o'clock news, I knew without a doubt in my mind something terrible would follow. In my experience it's very unusual for any electoral authority to issue such a public announcement to clarify a ridiculous error in the presence of 22 years of dictatorship. What do you expect would follow that? Jammeh would later use this error as the main pillar of his argument against the elections results.

On 2nd December 2016 after the IEC declared the coalition candidate Mr Adama Barrow as the winner of 2016 Gambia presidential elections, at 8 p.m. President Jammeh's message of congratulation, including his acceptance of the election results, was aired on the GRTS news:

"The outgoing President Yahya Jammeh, in a televised telephone call heard on state TV, congratulated president-elect Adama Barrow for his victory.

Both leaders exchanged pleasantries emphasising their desire to ensure a smooth transition of power.

"I hereby take this opportunity to congratulate President-elect Mr Adama Barrow, for his victory. It is a clear victory because our system says a simple majority," outgoing President Jammeh said, in his broadcast address to the nation, after the declaration of the election result.

"I wish him all the best and I wish all Gambians the best. As a true Muslim, who believes in Almighty Allah, I will never question Allah's decision.

"I came on a Friday on 22nd in the month of July 1994; today is Friday the 2nd of December 2016, you Gambians have decided that I should take the back seat; you have voted for somebody to lead our country and I wish you all the best."

Speaking directly to Barrow on mobile phone before he addressed the nation, Jammeh said: "I am calling you to wish you all the best; the Gambian people have spoken, and I accept the will of the Almighty Allah.

"I wish you all the best; the country will be in your hands in January, and you are assured of my guidance towards the transition, but you have to work with me as I pack to go to Kanilai after I have handed over the State House to you.

"You are the elected President of The Gambia and I wish you all the best. I have no ill will. Please ensure peace and stability, because without peace and stability – let me make it clear – you cannot make it anywhere in Africa. So I wish you all the best."

Mr Barrow, in his remarks, said his victory signifies hope, and a new era for The Gambia.

"I am humbled by the massive support showed by Gambians," he said.

Barrow registered his profound gratitude and support from Gambians for the historic victory, and promised to work hard to curtail unemployment and revitalise the economy.

"I congratulate every Gambian for the historic change, and I promise to work on the country's stagnant economy and unemployment," he said.

He also promised to foster and restore good relations and mutual ties with the international community, as he respects human rights and works with the press."

This is how some of the Gambian media expressed gratitude of President Jammeh's acceptance of the election results as well as giving their immediate recommendations to the incoming President:

"Congratulations president-elect, Adama Barrow, Friday 02 December 2016 marked a historical event in the annals of The Gambia, for nobody expected the defeat of President Jammeh and were surprised to hear him conceding defeat.

Jammeh should be commended for that move, which stabilizes the peace and tranquillity of the country. President-elect Barrow who will take office in January 2017 has a heavy task and challenges before him. Since he is the President-elect, Barrow should now be given befitting security teams, for both his house and himself.

First, his tasks are to nurture peace and tranquillity, as well as to ensure national unity and reconciliation among Gambians, restore democracy and respect for human rights, the rule of law, Gambians the judiciary, abolish draconian media laws, promote freedom of expression, ensure the state media promotes divergent views, restore bilateral cooperation with the EU, donors, and the Commonwealth, ensure better relations with the neighbouring countries, allow Gambians especially the Muslims to freely practise their religion without hindrance, especially for prayer festivities like Eid-ul Fitr, Eid-ul Adha and Yamul Ashura, when the moon is sighted in The Gambia or neighbouring countries unless necessary, and The Gambia should be maintained as a secular state, as stated in the Constitution.

The Barrow government should discontinue unnecessary and unexpected holidays or better still inform workers a few days before holidays are declared.

As regards the national cleansing exercise (Set settal), this could be continued, but during the day people and commercial vehicles should go ahead with their business, but those who fail to clean their environments should be penalised.

Also the new authorities should reintroduce the time of work from Monday to Thursday 8a.m to 4pm and on Friday from 8a.m to 12.30pm.

All political detainees should be released, including journalists such as Momodou Sabally, former DG of GRTS, and Bakary Fatty also of GRTS.

Nobody should be detained for over 72 hours without being charged or released as stated in the constitution, and long detention without trial as well as torture should be abolished.

A commission of enquiry should be set up to investigate if any public servant is doing business.

There should also be a commission of enquiry to investigate mysterious deaths that took place in the previous regime, especially the deaths of Ousman Koro Ceesay, former Finance Minister, Deyda Hydara in 2004, co-publisher of The Point newspaper, the disappearance of Chief Manneh of the Daily Observer in 2006, the killing in broad daylight of Omar Barrow of Sud FM on 14 April 2000 while reporting the student demonstration which claimed 14 lives, the death of Solo Sandeng, youth leader of the United Democratic Party, who died in custody in April 2016, and Ebrima Solo Krummah , who died at the EFSTH hospital, and so many other allegations of disappearances.

For all these the culprits should be brought to justice to face the full force of the law.

With the new government, prices of basic commodities and taxes should be drastically reduced; bills of electricity and water supplies should be reduced and distribution of such essential social amenities as water and electricity should be increased.

There should be rehabilitation of streets of the capital city of Banjul as well as the KMC, especially the feeder roads.

The ferry services should be improved upon with new ferries and landing fees of airlines should be reduced to encourage more international airlines, as presently it is a nightmare to travel by flight from The Gambia to the rest of the world, especially to our neighbouring countries.

In terms of sports, the government should endeavour to invest more in it, finance and develop the country's sports by training more sports personnel, athletes, technicians, etc to enhance the game.

Sport today is a crucial revenue base for any nation, and The Gambia is no exception.

The government should have meetings with the business community and foreign exchange bureau dealers and bankers, as well as economists to see the way forward to boost the economy.

Government should look into cases of most of the civil servants and officials of parastatals sacked, and those found faultless and competent should be reinstated.

The government should also invest more in agriculture to ensure the country is self-sufficient in food.

The government should build more hospitals and health centres, as well as improve the service delivery of health workers, especially in terms of the availability of medicines and modern equipment.

The new government should improve the quality of education in the country from basic to secondary and tertiary level.

It should be noted that according to the constitution, Barrow was voted in for a five-year term. Two-term limit should be introduced after his tenure.

If a minister is sacked, the reason should be made known to the public why he has been sacked.

All ministries and parastatals should have a public relations officer to facilitate access to information for the press.

A director of press should be appointed at State House to ensure all government press releases are sent to media houses, as well as organise frequent interviews or press conferences with the president and ministers to facilitate access to information."

During President Jammeh's tenure, the media and press were restricted in reporting freely and independently. Journalists faced the threat of harassment, imprisonment or even death if they reported anything which is critical to the government. There was a very limited cordial working relationship between the Gambian government and her citizens. As result most people view the government as the enemy of the people, with increased authoritarianism and dictatorship. On the other hand, the Gambian government viewed the citizens as useless, lazy and inadequate; they granted a very few basic human rights and freedoms to the citizens. This is why when Jammeh lost the election, the media, like everyone else, couldn't contain their joy.

Area	Coalition		APRC		GDC	
	Votes	%	Votes	%	Votes	%
Banjul	**6639**	**50**	5704	42	1028	8
Kanifing	**56107**	**50**	44873	40	11127	10
West Coast	74823	43	**76880**	**44**	21656	13
North Bank	**23346**	**37**	18316	29	22039	34
Lower River	**17646**	**56**	7996	27	5048	17
Central River	22215	32	**30228**	**43**	17581	25
Upper River	**28102**	**44**	24490	38	11289	18

This is the table of the 2016 Gambian presidential election result across the seven administrative areas throughout the country. Numbers in bold indicate the winning party in each area.

On 19th January 2017, President Elect Adama Barrow took the oath in the Gambian embassy in Dakar while he waited for President Jammeh to peacefully vacate the Gambia State House in Banjul:

'Fellow Gambians and Friends of the Gambia,

I am humbled to stand before you to address the whole world on this historic occasion. This is a day no Gambian will ever forget in one's lifetime.

This is the first time since The Gambia became independent in 1965 that Gambians have changed their government through the ballot box.

I must take this opportunity to thank the entire electorate of The Gambia and Gambians in the Diaspora for making this day possible.

I thank the entire campaign team of Coalition 2016 and the stakeholders for putting aside their political differences to unite us for the national interest.

Distinguished Ladies and Gentlemen,

Allow me to register special appreciation to Her Excellency Ellen Johnson Sirleaf, President of Liberia, and the Chairperson of Authority of Heads of States of ECOWAS, for her personal commitment and tireless efforts towards resolving the political crises in The Gambia.

The same sentiment goes to H. E. Muhammadu Buhari, President of the Federal Republic of Nigeria, H.E. Ernest Bai Koroma, President of the Republic of Sierra Leone and H.E. John Dramani Mahama, former president of Ghana.

I must also express profound gratitude to ECOWAS, AU, the Security Council of the United Nations and all friendly nations who stood by us during our time of greatest need.

I wish to thank His Excellency Macky Salla, President of the Republic of Senegal, and his government for their hosting and hospitality accorded me and my delegation at the request of the ECOWAS Chair.

This is what it means to be part of a Community of Democratic Nations.

Exceptional circumstance has compelled me to be sworn here today, and does not permit all those who made this day possible to be present.

It was later realised that the loser of the Election may not fulfil the mandate of a caretaker government, and facilitate a proper Inauguration with the full support of all state Agencies.

In fact, two days before the term of office of the incumbent expires a State of Emergency was declared.

However, the Constitution of the Gambia does not permit any lawmaker to deprive a citizen of a right that is already acquired. My right as a winner to be sworn in and assume the Office of President is constitutionally guaranteed and irreversible.

I hereby make a special appeal to ECOWAS, AU and the U.N. particularly the Security Council to support the Government and people of The Gambia in enforcing their will, restore their sovereignty and constitutional legitimacy.

I therefore call on all civilian and military Personnel of the state to support my Presidency since it is built on a Constitutional foundation.

They are assured that they will not be subjected to any injustice and discrimination, but would be provided with better working conditions and terms of service.

This is a victory of the Gambian Nation. Our National flag will now fly high among those of the most Democratic Nations of the world. The capacity to effect change through the ballot box has proven that power belongs to the people in The Gambia.

Violent change is banished forever from the political life of our country. All Gambians are therefore winners. There is no loser in the Gambian Election.

It is a fact that we contest Elections on the basis of political diversity but we build Nations on the basis of National Unity. We are here assembled as One Gambia, One Nation and One People.

Throughout our campaign we promised to unify our diverse people so that each would take ownership of the country, irrespective of ethnic origin, religion, gender or any other differences. Today, most Gambians are united in order to give Gambia a new start.

Hence, as of today, I am the President of all Gambians, regardless of whether you voted for me or not.

We could now become the architects of a Democratic Republic that is built on the pillars of Good Governance, Rule of Law and Respect for Fundamental Rights and Freedoms.

My government will implement comprehensive reforms. These include constitutional, institutional and legal reforms to expand the democratic gains we have made.

Your Excellencies, Honourable Guests, Fellow Gambians,

I belong to the generation of children who were born in 1965 when The Gambia became independent. I believe in the wise saying that "to whom much is given, much is expected".

I established a Think Tank, The Agency for Sustainable Socio-Economic Development (ASSED). This will bring experts on board to share their knowledge and skills in order to put in place an inclusive development agenda.

Your Excellencies, Honourable Guests and Fellow Gambians,

I would like to conclude by saying that men and women of this nation joined hands to effect a change that was in the making for many decades.

This is a change that should bring liberty and prosperity to everyone, and not to be discriminated on the basis of gender, religion or ethnic origin.

We are now determined to build a Gambia where merit and what you know counts more than who you know.

As the Commander-in-Chief of the Armed Forces, I call on all personnel of the Armed Forces and other security agencies to remain loyal to the Constitution and to the Republic.

I command the Chief of Defence Staff, and other officers of the High Command to demonstrate their loyalty to me as their Commander-in-Chief, without any delay.

I command all members of the Armed Forces to remain in their barracks. Those found wanting or in possession of firearms without my order, shall be considered rebels.

Gambia is our homeland! It demands our love and loyalty. Let us all pledge our affirm allegiance to be ever true to our motherland The Gambia; Long live the republic of the Gambia."

Note: by international law, the Gambian embassy in Dakar, Senegal, is technically Gambian territory. Due to the political crisis in the homeland, the President Elect took the oath there in order for him to be able to authorise any military intervention to Gambia which might be required to install him as the third President of the Republic.

On Saturday 18th February 2017, President Barrow formally took his inauguration oath on Gambian soil at the Independent Stadium, Bakau. He took the oath in the presence of the chief justice of the Gambia, Mr Hassana Jallow, witnessed by many thousands of Gambians, including me. Just to keep a record for the benefit of generations to come, I decided to include his full speech in this book:

My Colleagues, Heads of State and Governments,

Special Guest of Honour,

Your Excellences First Ladies,

Honourable Ministers,

Speaker of the National Assembly,

National Assembly Members,

My Lord Chief Justice,

Members of the Diplomatic and Consular Corps,

Venerable Religious and Traditional leaders,

Invited Guests,

Members of the Media,

Fellow Gambians,

May I begin by thanking Allah for making me the 3rd President of this great country through the support of the Gambian people; I seek guidance and blessing for me and my cabinet to have the strength and wisdom to serve our beloved nation to higher heights.

I would like to first of all welcome the distinguished heads of states and international guests who are here to share this joyous occasion with us.

Today is symbolic because of two important developments in the history of our dear motherland. It was on this day that The Gambia was declared Independent. I was just three days old. Now I am the President of the

Republic of The Gambia after 52 years of nationhood. Few people would have thought that I will be standing here today to address the nation.

I would like to thank the Gambian electorates for their astuteness. They exercised their civic rights in a peaceful and non-violent manner during the campaign, on Election Day as well as after the elections. I will not do justice without recognizing and expressing my sincere appreciation to the Gambian Diaspora. They spent time and resources to support my candidacy through the social media. They encouraged family members and friends to vote for me. This is a victory for democracy. It is a victory belonging to all Gambians. It is the decision of Gambians to change a Government which has entrenched itself through the ballot box. That has made it possible for us to gather here today.

I wish to take this opportunity to thank the Gambian people, ECOWAS, AU, The UN and all our international partners in general for supporting us at the most critical period of our history. This has ensured that democracy has a meaning to our people.

Gambia has changed forever. The people are fully conscious that they can put government in office as well as remove it. No government will ever be able to entrench itself against the will of the Gambian people. This is the lesson we must draw from the change that has been brought by the people.

We are now confronted with many challenges. We have inherited an economy that has declined because of political uncertainty. During the political impasse, businesses were shot down, offices and schools were closed. Foreign missions scaled down their staff, 50, 000 left the country and over 126, 000 became internally displaced.

People restricted their movements and the country became ungovernable. The country would have remained in such a situation if the new government did not succeed in finding a solution to the impasse.

Your Excellencies, Honourable Guests, Fellow citizens,

The Government under my Presidency will strive to ensure the survival, protection and development of all children.

The Ministry of Health and Social Welfare is charged with the responsibility of doing an inventory on the needs of the hospitals in the country in order to determine the inputs necessary to upgrade health services. It is to ensure staff audit in order to identify constraints and develop programmes to enhance staff motivation.

The Government will seek to partner with ECOWAS, AU, the UN, other traditional development partners like the US, the EU, UK and new development partners to improve on infant and maternal health. The aim is to improve their well-being and reduce mortality.

We will work to improve nutrition, sanitation, access to clean drinking water and ensure that primary health care is accessible and affordable to both rural and urban centres.

The law of the land instructs that basic education shall be free, accessible and compulsory. All Gambian children must go to school. The Gambia under my presidency will respect the dictates of the Constitution and work with our development partners to make free education for all a reality.

Agriculture shall be given added support to move towards food security and growth in export. Production and processing crops, livestock and fisheries will serve as the base for food security. These will be linked to job creation and increase in income through agro industrial development.

The service sector, which is now the largest contributor to the Economy, will be given necessary incentives to contribute towards employment creation and GDP growth.

Macro-economic stability will provide a fertile ground for telecommunication services, banks, hotels, insurance, housing companies and other sectors to grow and develop partnerships in Africa and all over the globe.

The Ministry of Information and Communication Infrastructure will be given support to sustain its local area networks. This will make it possible for the Government to maintain the regional community information centres and provide them with the necessary ICT services. The e-government data centre will create better coordination and cooperation between government institutions.

The media, both public and private, will enjoy freedom to disseminate divergent views and dissenting opinion as required by the Constitution. The Media Law shall be reviewed and code of conduct for responsible journalism promoted.

This will include re-orientation of the state media to take up its public service responsibility.

As part of the reforms to be undertaken to improve on job creation, e-government will be utilised to ensure that the Personnel Management Office and the Labour Department would be able to store data on those seeking employment and the jobs available at each given period. This will facilitate proper assessment of employment and unemployment rates especially among the young people. The Government will undertake a major drive to promote employment in all sectors.

In the area of infrastructural development the Government will give the Ministry of Works, Construction and Infrastructure time bound deadlines for the construction of the Basse-Fatoto, Fatoto-Koina and Laminkoto-Pasamas roads.

The ministry will undertake to identify all the key feeder roads in the country that require feasibility studies to prepare solid plans to source funds for their construction.

In the area of Energy, the ministry is charged with the responsibility of ensuring adequate and affordable electricity supply by diversifying energy sources for basic household needs. The energy sector would be improved. The development of port facilities, road infrastructure, river transport and other services will attract foreign direct investment at a larger scale.

The Ministry of Petroleum will focus on developing the potential to exercise control and direction over the seismic surveys being done to explore the potential for oil production in the country. Industrial production shall be expanded to include robust development of the mining sector and the processing of raw materials into value added goods.

Transparency will be shown in this area to enable the people to know all developments regarding the sector.

Civil Service Reform will be undertaken to link appointment to merit and income to performance.

A Ministry of Planning and Good Governance is to be established to facilitate and monitor the development and implementation of a blueprint for socio-economic development. The Provision of quality social services is the fundamental objective of the government under my Presidency.

This would require sustainable Macro Economic stability and growth.

This is why I established a Think Tank, The Agency for Sustainable Socio-Economic Development (ASSED). It is charged with the responsibility to establish an expert bank. This will provide data on the different expertise available to share their knowledge and skills. Their expertise will be tapped in order to put in place an inclusive development agenda.

Regional administration will be done by public servants not political appointees.

The pay and grading structure of the civil service will be reviewed and pensioners will also benefit from the reforms.

State enterprises are to be reviewed with the view to adopt policies that would ensure that they pay dividend to government instead of being a liability.

The Government will undertake key constitutional and legal reforms which will be highlighted in my first address to the National Assembly.

It intends to enforce constitutional provisions that are entrenched to protect the fundamental rights of the citizens. Orders have already been given for all those detained without trial to be released.

The Attorney General and Minister of Justice will receive information regarding all those who are arrested without being traced. An appropriate commission would be established to conduct inquiries into their disappearances.

A Human Rights Commission will be established without delay to complement the initiatives of the Attorney General.

The National Council for Civic Education will be provided with the facilities to conduct civic education to promote national reconciliation in collaboration with other organisations that are set up to promote national unity and reconciliation.

The judiciary will receive adequate support in terms of personnel and independence to enable it to deliver justice without fear or favour.

The Gambia during the impasse knows what solidarity means. Senegal has proven to be a friend in times of need. The people of Senegal hosted the people who fled and the government hosted me as President-elect and worked hand in glove with ECOWAS, The AU, UN and the international community in general to ensure that the verdict of the Gambian people is not violated.

In this regard, my first trip as a head of state will be to Senegal so that we could discuss and conclude on matters such as the SeneGambia bridge, our common borders, the status of the Senegalo-Gambian Secretariat and other outstanding issues. We want the relation between the two countries to be a model for African integration.

I would like to give special thanks to President Ellen Johnson Sirleaf, the Chair of ECOWAS, President Muhamadu Buhari of Nigeria, President Ernest Bai Koroma of Sierra Leone and former President John Dramani Mahama of Ghana who undertook the first mediation efforts.

I cannot conclude without adding the names of President Alpha Conde of Guinea and President Abdul Aziz of Mauritania who stepped in at the right time.

My special gratitude is also extended to my host President Macky Sall of the Republic of Senegal during the impasse. I was given a choice by ECOWAS to stay in Liberia, Nigeria or Senegal during the impasse.

I chose Senegal because of the fact we are the same people occupying two different countries. I must say I made the right choice and received the greatest hospitality.

Your Excellencies, honourable guests and fellow citizens, I would like to conclude by emphasizing that for 22 years the Gambian people yearned to live in a country where our diversity will be bridged by our tolerance and our determination to work together for the common good.

We decided to form a Coalition so that those speaking Jola, Serer, Aku, Serahuleh, Manjago, Mandinka, Fula, Wollof and all other groupings would ensure that we build One Gambia, One Nation and One People. Justice will guide our action and this Government intends to maintain that spirit of national unity.

The whole world supports us and The Gambia will remain a beacon of peace and hope for others to draw lessons from.

Long Live The Republic! Long Live the United People of The Gambia! Forward Ever! Backward Never!

The chief guest of honour to attend Gambia's 52nd

independence celebrations and the inauguration of President Adama Barrow, Senegal's President Mr Mack Sall, delivered a keynote speech to thousands of peoples at the Independent Stadium Bakau before the speech of President Barrow. The purpose of this speech is to serve as a reminder to the next generations of Africans that Gambians and Senegalese are one nation, one people:

Senegalese President Macky Sall has said The Gambia and Senegal would continue to work together in peace, stability and harmony to ensure that both nations build a strong foundation and legacy for generations to come. Mr Sall who is the chief guest of honour by President Barrow to attend the Gambia 52 Independent celebration as well Barrow Inauguration.

He made a remarkable speech in English on Saturday 18 February 2017 at the inauguration of President Adama Barrow and celebration of the 52nd independence anniversary of The Gambia, held at the Independence Stadium in Bakau.

He said "The Gambia and Senegal is one nation whose people were separated during colonial times; nevertheless, the two nations have continued to be one and the same in all ways". And add

"If you live in Senegal it is just like you are living in The Gambia, because the way of life is the same. There is no difference between the two nations ranging from culture to religion,"

He continues: "As far as we are living, we will continue to work in harmony and maintain that relationship our forefathers and grandparents were enjoying."

President Salla further congratulated the people of The Gambia for the peaceful change of government through the ballot box, and for waiting patiently for the political impasse to settle.

The following statement delivered by President Sall on his speech at Independent Stadium Bakau "that the two nations need peace, harmony, security, stability and development because these are the real challenges the two nations are faced with, if they continue to work hand in solve all these challenges will turn to strengths. The Gambia and Senegal are blood relatives. We are much more than one people; we are family just divided in to two states by circumstances of history. But we are inseparable because we shared the same value, the same wealth of life. We are bound by common history and common destiny. This is the legacy we received from our ancestors and our common duty is to build this legacy the foundation for better future. We owe it ourselves; we owe it to nest generation today more than ever from Banjul to Bargny from Brikama to Bingona and from Serrekunda to Tambakunda we are one family. What we need is peace, harmony, security and stability. What we need is development of our peoples. These are the real challenges of our time and that is the message that I carried from our brothers and sisters of Senegal."

Behind closed doors Mr. Sall has played a crucial role in bringing about the end to Jammeh regime. When he entered the stadium he received a rousing welcome from the jubilant crowd chanting his name.. Macky! Macky! Macky!

We should note that by the year 2016, diplomatic relations between the Gambia and neighbouring Senegal were at all-time low due to the frequent border closures. Each side blamed the other for not co-operating with the transportation rules and regulations of the country. President Jammeh in particular made a series of harsh remarks towards Senegal's authorities. At a meeting held in Farafenni, Jammeh threatened to teach Senegal's people a lesson if they didn't change their government and replace it with one that he would be able to work with. He frequently warned Senegal's regime about being aggressive towards the Gambia, and said they would regret such a stance. Consequently it became a priority for Senegal's government to remove Jammeh from power. The 2016 political impasse was a window of opportunity they could not afford to miss. Subsequently, due to diplomatic and military pressure from Ecowas, led by Senegal, Jammeh finally relinquished power on 20th January 2017.

So this entire chapter relates to statements and reactions during the Gambian political impasse, Friday 9th December 2016 to Friday 20th January 2017. At that time I was in the Gambia monitoring the political situation in the country, and

I travelled the country to gather fact and information in relation to the political impasse. I hope that by sharing this information with you, it gives you a basis you form your own conclusions about what happened. Additionally, it might serve as a record for future generations.

CHAPTER 6
LET'S REMOVE THE VEIL OF IGNORANCE

I know it's not going to be easy to reveal the true nature of the former Gambian President Yahya Jammeh, but we must do that to move forward. There is no doubt that Jammeh is the most controversial politician not only in the Gambia but in the whole of West Africa. I hope I am not getting on your nerves by continually talking about Jammeh and his regime. I think it's essential for Gambia as country to reach closure, and a satisfactory conclusion to the Jammeh era. By closely examining the regime which baffled Gambians for decades, we surely help the nation to turn the page to a new chapter, and open the door to prosperous future without looking back. However, it is almost impossible if Gambia as a nation doesn't vomit out what sticks in her chest from horrible experiences of the past, and make sure it never happens again.

I think if am going to be fair to Jammeh, I have to be honest about the following facts about modern civilisation. The 21st century political dilemma is this: people don't usually get to know the true identity of their leaders or their real intention towards the public.

When politicians give a speech to the public, they speak from notes, drafted by multiple speech writers. Whatever they utter is not their word, but somebody else's word. Before politicians speak, they usually gauge the public mood, which means their speech is designed to measure and match with public opinion. As a result the real nature of the politician is invisible to their electorate. President Jammeh is no exception.

I have to admit I was baffled for months when gathering accurate information about Jammeh and his government. Jammeh does not appear to have many personal or childhood friends. Additionally there are only a handful of his blood relatives in the Gambia, the majority of which are not known to the public. I think I can also safely argue that the majority of books published in the Gambia about to him and his government were like job applications. They didn't contain any clues about his personality, nor did they provide any useful information regarding his true character. Whoever wants to profile Yahya Jammeh has to rely on his speeches from video clips, as well as printed materials such as newspapers, government files, and his own diaries (if ever one could be found).

President Jammeh is a distinctive character who I think has displayed four different identities:

1: he successfully transformed himself from a common military officer to a devoted Muslim.

2: he gave the impression that he was a holy man with mysterious powers.

3: he pretended he was ignorant, while in reality he is very intelligent.

4: he showed the public that he was very tough, while in reality he is very insecure.

Let's ask ourselves why someone would display such bizarre behaviour. I'll use a little psychology to explain.

First of all, Jammeh is very intelligent politician who uses psychological dominance and political charisma to achieve what he wants and quickly gain people's trust.

Let's focus on how he successfully uses his first identity as a devoted Muslim to lure people in to a compromised position, where he can use his monopoly to control them as well as trick them to his advantage.

When he dealt with Muslims, particularly religious scholars, his physical image was a white Muslim dress and holding the holy Quran. People found his behaviour fascinating and it mesmerized the faithful and almost hypnotized them. Those who are naive and have religious convictions believed that Jammeh was innocent and he was incapable of doing anything harmful to anyone; it was just matter of time before he gained the trust of those people.

He sometimes used myth and superstition to gain control over those who believe in such practises. If you want to control a society where human affairs can be attributed to myths and supernatural events, it helps to mystify yourself by pretending to have supernatural powers and claiming to have connections with mythical beings. It's vital for one to use that monopoly on the faithful wandering in that particular wilderness. It helps you to control them, it will strengthening your position in that society, and attracts favours for you from those living in that spiritual fantasy world.

Monopoly works for Jammeh even if it means against himself; on an number of occasions he claimed that he is "not a politician"; in his own words, "politics is dirty game". However, he pursued and achieved most of his short and long term goals by using only political means and the political process, thanks to his physical and psychological monopoly.

Now let's focus our attention on Jammeh's use of charisma to control people. When he dealt with intellectual and intelligent people, he used his charisma in two ways. One: he would give them lavish gifts or rapid job promotions. Two: he would usually give the impression to people in high positions that he was ignorant. He used that method just to trick them to ensure they dropped their intellectual guard. This always worked to Jammeh's advantage. While they were comfortably sitting in the intellectual throne of Jammeh's government, imagining Jammeh as an idiot who is not smart enough to control such a mighty empire, without warning Jammeh would strike by sending some to prison, some disappeared without a trace, some went to exile in foreign lands and a lucky few merely got sacked from their jobs.

Jammeh uses his military skill to show to the security forces that he was both physically and psychologically tough. He uses his charisma as a deterrent to security personnel, some of whom might hold a grudge against him and his family. It worked perfectly for him. For almost 23 years while he sat on his throne; they dare not threaten either his personal life or the lives of his family, or his property.

In the scale where I measure human behaviour as well as capacity, on that index Jammeh belong to the category I call the "Kings Group". People who belong to this group would usually achieve all their goals by using charisma and a monopoly. Most of these people are both very lucky and naturally likeable. President Jammeh has those two main attributes.

Let's now explore human psychology from my little understanding of sociology. Can we firstly begin by asking the following big question: why do leaders from humble origins end up as dictators?

I think there are social factors as well as economic ones. Based on my own understanding I would say that hate and ignorance are the cause of all evil. Encouraging people to love one another, and educating people, will destroy all evil on earth. Dictatorship is a side effect of hate and ignorance.

I think there are only two type of dictatorship; a situational dictator or a circumstantial dictator. The five main continents on the earth are Africa, America, Europe, Asia, and Australia. Each country from each continent was once ruled by a dictator. Some were ruled by dictators many times until after the Second World War. If we collectively ask ourselves: do we need dictatorship in modern society? The correct answer would be no.

However, there are many underlying issues why dictatorships develop. No human being is born to be evil or a tyrant. Usually, due to a sequence of negative social and environmental experiences, they become evil. Peoples don't usually rise to power with the intention of becoming a dictator and an authoritarian; the political situation or personal and social circumstances create that.

In a society where social stratification and tribal loyalty is more prevalent and tribal interest is more superior to common interest, every single tribe would consider themselves more superior than others. As result in such a society people usually preferred to live by the rules of their own culture and tradition rather than any other common law. Such attitudes would create room to accommodate something I call a "situational dictatorship"; as we seen in the Gambian case; for anyone to lead such society; in order to maintain unity and stability, dictatorship seems inevitable. Perhaps dictatorship is an unfinished business in the Gambia as long as her citizens continue to hold on to old fashioned culture and traditional beliefs as well as pursuing tribal and religious interest.

Note: Guinea Conakry was twice ruled by dictatorship; first by Ahmed Sekou Toure from 1958 to 1984; and then by Lansana Conte from 1984 to 2008. Uganda was also ruled by dictator twice: by Idi Amin from 1971 to 1979 as well as current President Yoweri Museveni (1986 onwards). I can add Iraq to the list; Saddam Hussein's reign from 1979 to 2003 and subsequently Nouri Al Maliki from 2006 to 2014.

On the other hand, a society where religious and sectarian interest is more superior and prevalent then national interest, something which I call "circumstances dictatorship" would emerge, as we have seen in the Middle East, South Asia and the Gulf region. You can safely drop your own bombshell by asking the following question: "Yaya, then why there is no dictatorship in India and Brazil, where religious and caste stratification are more common than in Africa and the Middle East?"

Let's study India first. The massive difference in India is that the indigenous Hindu religion first created the caste system which accommodated all the tribes into one Hindu religious family. Eventually, Hindu religious interest exceeded all other interests and the caste interest became secondary: as result Hinduism became the common interest of all citizens. There was no vacuum for dictatorship because Hinduism is dictating everyone.

Brazil is different to India. Brazil as a country is a bunch of migrants from all over the world. The indigenous Brazilians have long disappeared into the wilderness. There is no internal pressure from anyone within the country to unify the people as well as desire for any other common interest. Individual tribes and religious groups are happy to live side by side without much social interaction. The room for dictatorship in such a society is minimal. Additionally the vacuum from slavery has mainly given power and leadership to only one social class which is widely seen to be acceptable by Brazilian society. This also pushes the country further from any type of dictatorship, in contrast to African and Middle Eastern countries.

In Africa, Christianity, Islam and modern democracy are all foreign concepts. Indigenous African people have established their rich culture and common interests long before Christianity, Islam and modern democracy; consequently the interests of indigenous culture and tradition are superior to all other interests. Hence it's difficult to accommodate modern civilisation without applying any form of dictatorship.

After the Gambian political impasse, dictated by the outcome of 2016 Presidential election, only then did the British government and media outlets label President Jammeh as a dictator. Why did they wait that long? Jammeh had long declared himself as a dictator for development. My theory is this; if the British government accepted Jammeh's dictator status long before the Gambian general elections, the British government would have been under too much pressure from the international community to remove Jammeh forcefully from power. However, after the 2016 presidential election, when Jammeh initially accepted the result and subsequently changed his mind, perhaps it was the opportunity for the British government to acknowledge his dictatorship status because they could now rely on the wider international community to force him out peacefully.

Another point of observation: can dictatorship be used as a positive term as well as a negative term? When Jammeh declared himself as a dictator for development, has such a thing ever existed? Why does someone like Jammeh, who is from a humble family background, end up being a dictator? I think the following fact contributed to this mystery; he might have felt insecure from security forces in his immediate surroundings and the lack of trust and loyalty from other tribes. As a result, he was in constant need of loyalty and assurances from different tribes as well as the army. Those were essential to his survival at whatever cost, even if it mean threatening lives and properties. Eventually he was disconnected from logic and rational thinking. If anyone said anything to him, it had to be measured to match with his psychological needs. That's exactly why when I sent him the following letter during the political impasse while I was in the Gambia:

"In every situation, there could be a positive outcome. May Allah bring that positive outcome to resolve our political nightmare very soon?

On the 2nd of December 2016, shortly after the IEC chairman announced the election result, I was overwhelmed with emotion and close to tears, especially when I heard that His Excellency President of Republic of The Gambia Sheikh Professor Dr Yahya AJJ Jammeh had conceded defeat and accepted the result.

I never thought Gambians were capable of such a miraculous decision. However, it does not surprise me because I always believed and had a lot of confidence in President Jammeh when he reiterated he is a God-fearing Muslim, and he will accept God's will and the will of the Gambian people.

At that moment, President Jammeh earned the universal respect not only of Gambians, but the international community, as well as his political opponents.

Not only me, but even some major media outlets such as BBC and FRANCE24 admitted that; because some foreign powers never believed that Gambia could conduct such a peaceful free and fair election, and democratically change their government without bloodshed or fear of the ruling elite.

This unprecedented move sparked a week-long celebration with euphoria which we never witnessed in The Gambia before. People like me do not celebrate that Jammeh lost the election and he is leaving office. However, we celebrate the maturity which Gambians showed to the international community; that we are intelligent and politically capable to implement our democratic process in line with international standards.

Additionally, the decency which President Jammeh demonstrated by appearing on national television, and called to congratulate the president-elect, Mr Adama Barrow, was fantastic.

Such landmark events indicated that The Gambia is unique in Africa, and it raises our expectation that there will be no hindrance to a peaceful transition to a new government.

It is also an opportunity for other countries to use The Gambia as a role model, and an example in Africa.

As a Muslim, I feel guilty without taking action to express the way I felt. I am, therefore, personally appealing to President Yahya AJJ Jammeh and his entire government to maintain his previous position, by ensuring a peaceful transition to President-elect Adama Barrow.

Sir (Jammeh), I know you love The Gambia and you have a good heart for this country; it's almost impossible to list the many great things which you have done for this country.

In my previous article, which was published in the Daily Observer, I have highlighted the number of development projects which you have undertaken since 1994.

In addition, you are a role model to many young people around the world. I remember when I was in Sydney, Australia, last year. I met a man from Sudan, who asked me where I'm from. When I told him I came from The Gambia, he embraced me and said, "How is your president Yahya Jammeh? A true pan-Africanist; I really like him."

Many Gambians are familiar with such remarks from people in the Diaspora. The legacy of great leaders like you will last for many centuries to come. You served The Gambia for almost 23 years.

Our holy Prophet Muhammad (PBH) served his Ummah for almost 23 years. There are many great examples like this in the past. You can rest assured that the development foundations which you have planted in this country will never be uprooted.

Long live the Republic of The Gambia; let's maintain the peace and stability. One Gambia, One People."

The above letter was published in some Gambian local newspapers, for example the Point newspaper published on 5th January 2017, as well as the Gambia online news. If you notice all that I stated in the letter was fact, based on my own personal experience. However, it's carefully designed for someone who wouldn't listen to you if you didn't praise him or acknowledge his mighty status. I think I am vindicated by Jammeh's own former speaker of the national assembly, Madam Fatoumatta Jahumpa Cessay, in the following letter which she sent to Jammeh during the same period of Gambian political impasse. This is what she says to him, published in the Point newspaper on Tuesday 3rd January 2017:

Fatoumatta Jahumpa Cessay, a former Speaker of the National Assembly under the Government of President Yahya Jammeh, has asked President Jammeh to accept the result of the December 1 Presidential election, and agree on "a peaceful, dignified and amicable exit" for President-elect Adama Barrow to assume office come January 19 this year.

Now a Consultant on Gender/Children; Governance; Elections; Parliamentary and Peace/Conflict Resolution, Mrs Jahumpa Cessay, who has been a visible and strong advocate for the development plans, policies and mission of the APRC party, stated: "…With utmost respect and great affection for you, your family and the Gambian people, I believe strongly that it will be in the supreme interest of our people, our country, sub-region and for the preservation of your handsome legacy, to work with your colleagues in ECOWAS, as well as the AU, UN, OIC, EU, Gambia Bar Association (GBA), Gambia Chamber of Commerce and Industry (GCCI), your current serving ambassadors, civil society groups, including religious, women, youth and student groups, as well as the security chiefs; to agree on a peaceful, dignified and amicable exit for you in a manner befitting of a Head of State. This will make way for the President-elect to continue the work that you have started."

The statement of Mrs Jahumpa Cessay, commonly known as FJC, is as

131

follows:

ON THE POLITICAL IMPASSE IN THE GAMBIA

Your Excellency, Sir, please accept warmest fraternal greetings from me and on behalf of my family; to you Mr. President and to Her Excellency First Lady Madam Zineb Yahya Jammeh and to first family. As we have just celebrated the birth of the Prophet (SWT), Jesus Christ (RA) and we prepare to welcome the New Year, I first want to take this early opportunity to pray for your continued good health and long life Your Excellency, and that of your family and all Gambians.

I wish to rededicate my commitment to your great vision to make the Gambia a modern country and one of the leading nations in Africa and throughout the world. I further want to reaffirm my unfaltering support for these plans and to pledge to you that the mission will be completed Insh Allah, whilst wishing you a happy and prosperous 2017 in advance. I also want to seize the same opportunity Your Excellency, to thank you for the opportunities that you gave to me and my family, as well as to the many Gambians, to contribute, in our small way, to the massive development and progress you have brought to the people of the Gambia in the twenty two years of your rule.

My family and I will forever be grateful to Your Excellency for your generosity and your great vision.

Sir, personally, I owe you a great debt of gratitude, because you gave me the opportunity to represent my country in the great offices of our nation, the sub-region of West Africa, the African Continent and beyond. It is during your glorious tenure that I ascended the high offices of the Speaker of the National Assembly, First Female Deputy Speaker of the ECOWAS Parliament, President of the Commonwealth Parliamentary Association, and as Your former Director of Press and Public Relations and now a Consultant on Gender/Children; Governance; Elections; Parliamentary and Peace/Conflict Resolution.

I have also been a visible and strong advocate for the development plans, policies and mission of our great party the APRC to transform the Gambia into a middle income country in the shortest possible time. So thank you, Your Excellency, for laying a firm foundation for a modern Gambia, in just 22 years and for the good fortune you bestowed on me. Your great achievements as President of the Second Republic are already documented in history and you have in the process, carved an indelible place for yourself in the history of our great nation. It is with a deep sense of foreboding, Your Excellency that I write this plea addressed to Your Excellency, as a former Speaker of the National Assembly, and in my personal capacity as a private citizen of the Gambia and as Peace and Development Advocate with special interest in the welfare of Women/Children and Good Governance. I write it with the clear knowledge of the consequences of civil conflict on our women and children, and it is this that I respectfully ask Your Excellency to reflect on at this most difficult time in our country's history, as you prepare to exit in grace and dignity.

Having said that Your Excellency and following extensive consultation, several concerned people, both inside and outside of the Gambia have asked for my personal intervention in this political impasse that ensued after the Presidential election of 1st December 2016, in which Mr. Adama Barrow was elected as incoming President, in a free and fair election.

I must appeal to you Your Excellency and my dear brother, that my pride and elation in you and your family knew no bounds upon hearing the glowing tributes and respect that were lavished on you specifically and to the Gambian people generally; when you graciously conceded defeat and publicly congratulated the President-elect Mr Adama Barrow for his handsome victory

Therefore, on the 2nd of December 2016, you added yet another achievement to your many other achievements, by showing the world that the Gambia is a democracy and Gambians are democratic, and we can have a peaceful transfer of power through constitutional means. You confounded the critics and impressed the world with your mature gesture of magnanimity in defeat and proved once again that you are a true democrat, a true Pan-Africanist and a devout Muslim in faith.

Your Excellency in your televised congratulatory telephone call to President-elect Mr. Barrow, you graciously informed him that his victory is the decision of Allah (SWT) and that you believe in whatever Allah decrees. To that end let me remind you, most respectfully of the long standing adage that, "Man proposes and God decides", so your unwavering belief in Allah (SWT), must now convince you that Allah is

133

Raheem and it is HE who controls our fates. Your Excellency, being born and bred in a family that is endowed with proven political pedigree, I understand the idea of winning and losing electoral contests.

Therefore, with utmost respect and great affection for you, your family and the Gambian people, I believe strongly that it will be in the supreme interest of our people, our country, sub-region and for the preservation of your handsome legacy, to work with your colleagues in ECOWAS, as well as the AU, UN, OIC, EU, Gambia Bar Association (GBA), Gambia Chamber of Commerce and Industry (GCCI), your current serving ambassadors, civil society groups, including religious, women, youth and student groups, as well as the security chiefs; to agree on a peaceful, dignified and amicable exit for you in a manner befitting of a Head of State.

This will make way for the President-elect to continue the work that you have started.

I wish to further suggest that you and the President–elect co-chair such a meeting of stakeholders, similar to what is being done in Ghana currently. Such an arrangement will further underscore your credible claim of putting the Gambia first in all your actions and intentions. Your Excellency, this action will also cement your commitment to the protection and preservation of the 1997 Constitution of the Gambia, to which you swore an

oath of allegiance, in which you pledged to execute your obligations under that constitution without fear, favour, affection or ill will, whilst upholding that Oath of Office.

I truly believe Your Excellency that if you listen objectively to your colleagues in ECOWAS, tasked with facilitating a peaceful transfer of power to President–elect Barrow, you will find agreement that will preserve the peace and avoid conflict. Your Excellency, Sir, my dear brother, I happily recall your often quoted statement that the women, the children and the youth, are your number one priority in your development blueprint. As a woman and child rights advocate; and on behalf of these vulnerable groups, please Sir do all that is in your God given powers to avert violent conflict, such as those that have claimed the lives of thousands of women and children in our sub-region in the last three decades and destroyed their future prospects. This I hope will never happen in the Gambia under your sterling Presidency of our beloved country.

Your Excellency please be rest assured of my continued support and prayers, as you work with your peers and your citizens, to find a peaceful resolution to this political impasse. You are fond and proud of saying that when you came in 1994, not even a chicken was killed. I hope as you exit the government, that the same be said of your exit, this time, may it be said that not even a fly was swatted.

Finally Your Excellency, let me pray that in this work may Allah (SWT) strengthen your will and your hands to reach a peaceful exit following your glorious tenure of 22 years. Please be further assured Your Excellency, of my continuous high regards and affection for you and your family. May God bless you, the First Lady H.E. Madam Zineb Yahya Jammeh and your beautiful children Mariam and Muhammed Jammeh;

Season's greetings and God bless you all.

Affectionate

Hon. Dr. Mrs. Fatoumata Jahumpa Ceesay.

In both letters to Jammeh, you can feel the agitation in our voice, like a kidnap victim in Isis-controlled Raqqah, blindfolded, hands tied behind his back, falling on his knees, begging the caliphate to spare his life. However to Jammeh this is nothing more than adulation.

How can someone be called a dictator? The meaning of dictator in simple English is whoever governs and rules the country without taking account of other people's opinions, and not having respect for, and due diligence to, the rule of law in the land. A widely held belief is that whoever stays in office for more than two five year terms was a Class A dictator: I think that notion is really not accurate.

If Jammeh falls under this category then truly he is a dictator; but for Jammeh supporters, he isn't. For them, he is none other than Gambia's savour from neo-colonialism and Senegal's aggression.

And my opinion of what constitutes dictator status? I think

it's entirely dependent on the political class you belong to. If you belong to the hereditary monarchical or royal family ruling elite in the Gulf and Europe, you are classed as royal family, and you are entitled to do whatever you like because of the divine rights of kings. If you in the good books of western supporters, like certain leaders in Asia and Africa, you are none other than a friend and ally who is democratically elected to serve their interest.

In this particular debate, you can come to your own conclusions.

The other day while on Facebook I saw a post from someone which said the following: "Is it strong countries that build strong institutions or is it strong institutions that build strong countries?"

I think this is similar to the old fashioned question related to the chicken and the egg; but simpler to answer. It reminds me what President Barack Obama said when he visited Ethiopia on 26thJuly 2015 - "what Africa needs is strong institutions, not strong leaders". Let's use the house as an example: before one can start building a house, first and foremost you need land and solid ground, which is the foundation for anything meaningful. To build the strong institutions in any country, first of all you need a strong sovereign nation, eventually strong institutions will follow.

The first moral duty for any citizen should be to understand what being a patriotic citizen means. Secondly; as John Kennedy put it "ask not what your country can do for you, ask what you can do for your country." This is the most fundamental attribute to any national development initiative. Building the essential institutions such as agriculture, health and education would eventually follow. We as Africans should be inspired by the rapid advances of western societies where citizens are proud of their citizenship. Western citizens are more aware of the dangers which lie ahead if they compromise their patriotism; such a precaution is the philosophy behind rapid Western development in building strong institutions.

In order for Africa and her citizens to attain superpower status in the modern world, we need to take ownership of our continent economically, intellectually and democratically as well as individually strive to contribute to nation building without hindrance from tribalism, religious conflicts, civil wars and lack of leadership. For instance in the United Kingdom if a restaurant waiter wins a £10 million lottery jackpot, he or she would automatically climb the social ladder from working class to become middle class. Equally if a street cleaner breaks the law, he or she will receive a punishment equal to those of the upper class, in contrast to the tribal system in Africa, the sectarian line in the Middle East, and the Indian caste system. The flexibility in social mobility as well as fairness in the justice system makes it possible for all citizens to firmly hold tight to citizenship; in such a society there will be no shortage of patriotism and loyalty in building the nation and her strong institutions.

We should note that radical groups such as skinheads, as well as minority Muslims and Christian religious fundamentalists, believe that black people are not capable of looking after their own affairs. Such a view is still very common in some parts of America and Europe. Perhaps I think such ignorance is due to the following negative attribute to blacks such as: black soul, black list, black sheep, black magic, black market, black etc. You can count such negative 'black' attributes in hundreds of sentences and phrases. Hence black people lack self-esteem and the confidence to dream big and achieve all their goals.

If you combined the entire world mineral resources underground and on the earth's surface, perhaps Africa has the largest resources of all: crude oil, gold, diamond, silver, uranium, fertile land and much more. Africans should not doubt that God loves Africa. If a father shares his will amongst his children, the one who received the most from him is the one whom he loves the most. Africa and other continents are siblings from the same father and that father decided to give the most to Africa because he dearly loves Africa.

During the 2016 Gambian political impasse, there were many millions of calls for President Jammeh to relinquish power peacefully to President Elect Barrow. I think I managed to read 90% of them! However, a letter from one James Mendey captured my imagination and resonated with more than any other: to me, the way he expressed his message to the country is how patriotic citizens should address their nation and her leaders, particularly during times of crisis. The letter might also serve as inspiration to the coming generations. The way Mr Mendey expresses his opinion while appealing to the head of state, and particularly the manner in which he chooses his words in the letter, has motivated me to share it with the readers of this book. I cannot resist the temptation do so.

Mr James Mendey's letter to President Jammeh published in the Froyaa newspaper on Tuesday 20th December 2016:

"The Gambia is at a very critical stage that calls for a general concern. We should not pretend as if things are alright. This is not the time to think about money or position but a time to give thought to our country and lovely people. Position comes and goes, money gets finished but our people remain our people. Our next world which is eternal also depends on our deeds on earth and not money or position.

At this crucial time, it is not a matter of who one supports or not. It is not a matter of differentiating our positions. This is not a time for discrimination, ethno centrism or politics. It is a time for all of us to work together as Gambians for a common goal irrespective of our religion, ethnicity, social status, culture or political opinion.

These are questions we Gambians should honestly answer with the fear of God. Is there any single Gambian who is more Gambian than the other? Should we not listen to each other with love as Gambians? Do we pay ourselves for our jobs or does the ordinary Gambian tax payer pay us, including poor farmers and labourers whose lives our actions may destroy including their families and children.

We have to critically think and see if anything is worth risking , eventually destroying the precious lives of our own parents, brothers, sisters and many other relatives, friends, including our own lives, our wives and husbands. Should we destroy all we have because of things that will not last? I call on all Gambians to approach this issue with either true love for our country or trust and honesty. A peaceful solution is in our hands, we just have to be frank to avoid violence, the consequence of which can be very devastating and only lead us to regret. We should learn from Burundi, Rwanda, DRC etc.

I call on religious leaders and elders to intervene in this matter with faith and honesty without fear. Considering the plight of all Gambians this is the right time and don't wait until it is too late. The government of the Gambia should critically think of the concerns raised here and so many other concerns and not assume that peace in The Gambia is entirely in their hands. They either save the precious lives of Gambians, their own people or render them vulnerable to possible destruction.

This is the time that everyone should choose between money, position and eternity. For the military the peace of the very tax payers who are paying our salaries is entirely in your hands, especially at this critical time. A very high level of professionalism and a very cordial civil military relation is much expected of you.

I thank all Gambians for the present stage of calmness despite all the challenges. Special thanks to president Elect Barrow and the entire coalition team for their success of maturity which demonstrates their concern and love for our country. I also thank the government of the Gambia and all the security forces for the security and present peaceful atmosphere.

The Gambia is our own so let us work as one people and nature the peace that we have. I strongly appeal to president Jammeh to please think of the precious lives of the thousands of Gambian children, Gambian youths, and women whom he had always mentioned in his speeches. Also the visually impaired and persons with disability should be considered. Let him also think of the infrastructural development achieved in the past years.

We are all Gambians and I appeal that he joins all Gambians in their decision in opting for a new president to whom he is an asset for advice. Please don't allow anything to deviate you from your frankness and you have for your people as manifested in your result acceptance. President

Jammeh, please hear the voice of ordinary Gambians and lead us to a peaceful transition."

In conclusion to this chapter before we collectively turn to the next, I would like to ask the most ridiculous question. Will former President Yahya Jammeh ever return to the Gambia? If yes, when and how?

Honestly, I have to admit, I am already missing Jammeh's eccentric personality. I can vividly remember when I saw him at 9 p.m. on Saturday 21st January 2017, leaving the Gambia at Banjul international airport, going to exile in Equatorial Guinea. A medium-sized African man, built like me, dressed in a Marabout waranboo, all white from head to toe, holding the holy Quran in his right hand, while additionally hanging on to a mysterious multi-coloured stick in his left hand, looking as confident as an innocent child, walking firmly like desperate coach on a football pitch and looking from side to side like someone who is competing in the London marathon. He appeared more heroic than fugitive.

As I said in Chapter One; back in 1993, when I was just 17 years old, I predicted there would be a military government in the Gambia. The 1994 military coup vindicated me.

Back in 2012, I made a similar prediction that Jammeh would appoint certain people to his cabinet. He did exactly as I predicted; except for one person who rejected his cabinet offer.

Very recently, in late November 2016, one week before the presidential election, I made three more predictions. My first was that if the election is free and fair, the incumbent president Jammeh would only win 32 to 35% of the popular vote, the opposition candidate Adama Barrow would win 40 to 45%, and the GDC's Mamma Kandeh would win 17 to 21%. I also thought that sooner or later, Jammeh would reject the election result.

The action he took on 9th December 2016 vindicated me on that. I was certain that in order for him to stay in power, President Jammeh would use every available intimidation method at his disposal to scare Gambians; however through international pressure I was sure he would eventually back off and step down. I was right, wasn't I?

I thought that Jammeh would not hide and run to exile; whatever he did, he would make sure it happened in full view of the public; and on 21st January 2017, he did exactly that.

With my successful record up to this point, I think once again I can safely give you the following predictions on Jammeh:

In the next three years or so, perhaps let's say until the next Gambian general election, Jammeh will try to launch his comeback to the Gambia. If he fails politically he will try to use other means. Let me explain how that is going to occur. You notice that since he left the country in January, he has been very quiet, but he won't be quiet for long. Maybe weeks from now, or months, but definitely not years, he will break that silence.

I think the first method he will use is he will release some ridiculous statement through his friends in the media in which he will try to apologise to Gambians for everything he did in the past 22 years. However, he will justify some of his actions and it's almost guaranteed that he will blame institutions such as the National Intelligent Agency, the military junta and the fortune tellers for his shortcomings.

Also he is likely to launch some sort of security sabotage against the state, and consequently peoples will yearn for Jammeh's strong type of leadership. However, he is going to have to be more manipulative and use completely different tactics to trick the military into backing him again.

The third method he will use, which is highly unlikely but is still possible, is that Jammeh would appeal to the Gambian government via international organisations like the UN, AU, Ecowas and the EU to try to negotiate some sort of amnesty for him to safely return back to Gambia as a private citizen.

Apart from the above mentioned scenarios, there are few possibilities which could bring Jammeh back to Gambia. The

APRC might form a coalition with other political parties in the Gambia and win an election, and that would mean Jammeh could come back. Or, after the findings of the upcoming Truth and Reconciliation commissions are published, if Jammeh is not deemed to pose any security threat to the nation, the Gambian government might extend amnesty, allowing him and his family to return home.

The worst case scenarios for Jammeh are the following three dilemmas.

1: If the pressure mounts from human rights groups on the international community and the Gambia government to indict Jammeh to face prosecution for his human rights violations.

2: If the government of Equatorial Guinea suddenly changes and he is no longer welcome there.

3: Or, God forbid, if he faces a life-threatening illness and his health suddenly deteriorates then Jammeh's future as well as all my predictions would head into a different dimension.

However, Jammeh will never be quiet and disappear into the wilderness like other exiled dictators. He will do whatever he can humanly do to try and come back to Gambia to rewrite his history in more favourable terms. Until then, don't be surprised if you see him rendering humanitarian assistance to conflict zones such as Syria, Iraq and other military conflict areas and war zones around the world.

He might take on further studies to become a medical doctor, or volunteer to engage in charity works. Unfortunately, as Liberian President Madam Ellen Johnson Sirleaf stated on BBC Focus on Africa "Jammeh being the person who he is" (she was reacting to Jammeh's break of diplomatic protocol during the political impasse when he record their phone conversation without her knowledge, and it was later broadcast live on GRTS), predicting what someone like Jammeh will do now is almost impossible and we all can propose many different theories.

We can view some examples from other countries. There are some similarities with Jammeh and the former Iranian leader Mohammad Reza Shah, who was forced from power by civil disobedience and went to exile in Egypt; however, due to his poor health a few years later he died in exile before having any chance to launch a comeback to power. The current Nigerian President Muhammad Buhari, once ruled Nigeria from 1983 to 1985. He managed to launch a comeback and successfully win the 2015 presidential election. The former Ugandan dictator Idi Amin, who was forced from power by a neighbouring country, died in 2003 while in exile in Saudi Arabia; he never attempted to make a comeback.

Another example is Guinea Bissau's former President Joao Bernardo Vieira: after he was deposed from power he went into exile for few years and successfully managed to make a comeback from 2005 to 2009, before he was brutally assassinated by factions within his military opponents.

It's prevalent for exiled leaders around the world to try and make a comeback to power. The practice is most common in Africa and the Middle East, but it's never been a smooth transaction for many. It's risky as well as dangerous. There is no doubt in my mind that former President Yahya Jammeh, if he is continues to be healthy, will try his luck to make a comeback to power. We shall wait and see.

It's time for Africa and her leaders to realize that there is a lot one can achieve as well as contribute to human society without occupying political office. One such example is Mrs Oprah Winfrey; she is among the top US talk show hosts and TV personalities; equally she is one of the most successful black women that ever lived. She made certain valuable remarks for those who wanted be successful: "Understand the next moment and seize your opportunities. Everyone makes a mistake: learn from your mistakes and work hard on yourself. Run the race as hard as you can; believe that we are all seeking the same thing. Find your purpose, stay grounded, relax, it's going to be okay."

It's essential for one to hold firm on those principles, and try to apply them to every aspect of your life, and surely one day you will be successful like Oprah Winfrey.

Africa, and particularly black Africans, will achieve very little if they continue to hold on the old fashioned belief systems such as putting all their faith in politics and the political process. If they fail, they put all the blame for their failure on European colonialism and politicians.

People must start to take responsibility for their own lives and be willing to work hard without relying on others; the concept of depending on others to improve our country and economy for us should belong to the past. There are no more effective weapons than logic and rational thinking. Before God, all human beings are equal. What make us unique and different are our geographical locations, and our determination to improve our lives and make the world a better place for all. My African environment and your European environment are all operating in the same atmosphere; however; the way to achieve more in life totally depends on your positive outlook and the way you view the world. If you're optimistic, you think "if I try harder, anything is within my reach". If you're pessimistic, you think "I don't have to work hard because God has already determined my destiny. I have to wait for God to provide everything for me on my plate. If I manage to achieve anything, it's thanks to God. If I fail, it's satanic influence, and nothing to do with me."

These concepts are what determine our future, good or bad.

CHAPTER 7
HOW CAN GAMBIA ATTAIN ECONOMIC SUPER-POWER STATUS IN AFRICA?

It will not be possible for the Gambia to attain economic superpower status in Africa if the country fails to learn from its past mistakes. Each chapter of this book is a valuable lesson which can bring the country a step closer to being an economic super power in the sub-region with an everlasting democratic process and the rule of law. The democratic dispensation which removed 22 years of dictatorship is a marvellous example, not only for Africa but the whole world. Gambia has strongly indicated to the world that Gambians are more political mature than the international community previously thought. The Gambia is in a strong position in Africa, which one could argue is equal to the status of ancient Greece, the birthplace of modern democracy. The new political dispensation in the country must ensure they do not follow in the footsteps of the past regime, by ensuring they put an end to the arbitrary arrests and government witch-hunts against political opponents. The new administration should make sure they immediately start to undertake the establishment of effective democratic institutions like an independent judiciary, a strong and effective legislative system, and sustainable economy policies including viable civic education to enhance citizens understanding of politics.

The new administration must re-evaluate Gambia's relationship with the International Criminal Court. The previous administration under Jammeh attempted to withdraw Gambia from the ICC, a decision I applauded at the time because the ICC mostly pursued leaders from African and Eastern European countries, while leaders from developed countries who committed heinous crimes and international aggression were never indicted by the ICC to face justice, e.g. Tony Blair and George W. Bush. Most international human rights groups believed the decision of the duo on Iraq constituted a war crime against humanity.

However, so far no attempt has been made to bring them to face justice. How come? It's one rule for the poor and another for the rich.

In the 70s, 90s and more recently, the governments of Burma, Algeria, Cambodia, and Zimbabwe all denied the victory of the opposition in their countries. As result the citizens of each of those countries experienced death and brutal torture due to election disputes. However, the international community as well as their regional blocks failed to intervene to restore democracy in those countries. Gambians at every level should appreciate the efforts of Ecowas, the UN, EU and AU for the decisive decision they took to prevent any single drop of blood in their country. Timely military peaceful intervention stopped the country from plunging into senseless civil war. I think it must be the moral duty of every Gambian to join with international political institutions, rights groups, and pressure groups for advocating and promoting human rights, democracy and good governance around the world. Gambia marks a beginning for the international community to reinforce democracy and the rule of law upon the government of any country in the future who might refuse to respect the will of its citizens. Thus I think it's essential for Gambia to observe every 2nd December as Gambia Freedom Day and every 20th January as Gambia Liberation Day.

For the benefit of our future generation; these are the statement made by the international community during the 2016 political impasse.

On Tuesday 20th December 2016, western countries, via their representatives in the Gambia, jointly delivered a press release on the Gambian political impasse:

The Ambassadors of the United Kingdom, the United States of America, the European Union, and the Chargée d'Affaires of Spain welcome the clear and unequivocal communiqué on the situation in The Gambia taken at the 50th session of the ECOWAS Heads of State and Government in Abuja on 17 December.

We fully support the eight points of agreement and specifically welcome the appointment of Presidents Buhari and Mahama as Mediator and Co-Mediator.

We further support the appeal for all stakeholders, within and outside The Gambia, to exercise restraint, respect the rule of law and ensure the peaceful transfer of power ends.

Later on Tuesday 20th December 2016, the French president also urged Jammeh to accept the result:

French President Francois Hollande on Tuesday urged Gambia's president of 22 years, Yahya Jammeh, to accept defeat in elections and stand aside.

Hollande said the results of the December 1 polls were "indisputable" and Jammeh's challenger Adama Barrow "must be installed as soon as possible".

"The matter is non-negotiable," he said after a meeting in Paris with visiting Senegalese President Macky Sall, whose country nearly surrounds Gambia.

He said he was confident Nigeria's President Muhammadu Buhari, who is mediating in the dispute on behalf of West African leaders, would "make the Gambian president listen to sense, and that the transition of power will take place peacefully on January 19."

"Otherwise we will have to enforce the sovereign decisions" taken by the 15-member Economic Community of West African States (ECOWAS), he warned.

Earlier Ecowas warned Jammeh to consider his options:

ECOWAS said Jammeh must step down next month when his term runs out and vowed "to take all necessary action to enforce the results" of the December 1 poll, without spelling out what those measures might be.

This is how the UN reacted:

Wednesday 14th December 2016, the UN representative in West Africa fury at Jammeh rejection of election result. He said: Gambian President Yahya Jammeh will not be allowed to remain head of state if he refuses to go after his elected term ends next month, and will face strong sanctions if he clings to power, the top U.N. official in West

Africa warned Jammeh.

"For Mr. Jammeh, the end is here and under no circumstances can he continue to be president. By that time (Jan. 18), his mandate is up and he will be required to hand over to Mr. Barrow," Mohammed Ibn Chambas, U.N. Special Representative for West Africa and the Sahel, told Reuters.

He adds Jammeh would be "strongly sanctioned" if he did not step down and hand over power to Barrow, without giving details.

Chambas accompanied a delegation of presidents representing the regional bloc ECOWAS who travelled to Gambia on Tuesday but failed to reach a deal that would see Jammeh step down.

Instead, Gambian soldiers seized the headquarters of the national elections commission and sealed it off just hours before the presidents touched down in the riverside nation.

United Nations Secretary-General Ban Ki-moon said that the takeover of IEC headquarters by Gambia security forces was an "outrageous act of disrespect of the will of the Gambian people".

During the period of political impasses the building in the capital Banjul remained deserted on aside from two armed security guards key locations in the town. Most front gates of government buildings and ground floor entrances were closed.

On Wednesday 18 January 2017 No one has gone to work. The chairman of IEC before fled to Senegal said" I didn't even try no one has informed me that I can go back," elections commission chairman Alieu Momar Njai.

Meanwhile APRC still hopes for some miracle from court. However, the court has not held a session for a year and a half, and legal experts believe that at least four new judges would need to be hired to hear Jammeh's petition.

"We do not believe it will be heard by a credible court dedicated to ensuring the integrity of The Gambia's democratic process," a U.S. Embassy statement said.

At the time; analysts have suggested that the challenge in the Supreme Court - the legal channel for resolving election disputes - could put diplomats in a difficult position.

While such disputes are relatively common in Africa, the international community generally defers to established domestic legal mechanisms for resolving them.

However, in a notable exception, U.N. troops intervened militarily alongside France to oust Ivory Coast's then-president Laurent Gbagbo after he used the constitutional court to overturn the 2010 election victory of Alassane Ouattara.

Asked whether military intervention was an option in Gambia if mediation failed; Chambas said: "It may not be necessary. Let's cross that bridge when we get there"

Note that the condemnation from the international community of Jammeh strengthened the positions of Gambians as well as boosted the morale of the coalition. Within a matter of days almost every major institution in the country publicly went to see Adama Barrow and pledged their support to his incoming government. This included health institutions, education institutions, religious leaders, the Gambia Bar Association, 11 Gambian ambassadors, individual businessmen, and representatives of the many industries in the country. The only institutions that remained loyal to the former president at that stage were the security forces, plus legislative, cabinet, and regional governors.

My personal encounter with President Barrow

I first meet President Adama Barrow very briefly to congratulate him on his election victory at his Yaram-Bamba residence on the coastal road on Wednesday 7th December 2016 at 9 p.m. two days before the political impasse began. Meanwhile I read his biography on the newspaper which indicated that among his hobbies is reading. While going to see him with two of my friends, Lai Suwareh and Kanjura Kani (or KK), I took two books with me. On our arrival there was a large jubilant crowd gathered at the gate of his compound, all desperate to see him. However I was lucky to have KK with me; he is a prominent member of the UDP in London, and as a result I got easy access to the President-elect. Shortly before we met him, while waiting in his living room, I noticed two people sitting on my left hand side. When I turned around, I realised it was Hajratu Fatoumatta Tamajang (who later became the vice-president and Minister of Women's Affairs) and Dr Isatou Touray (who later became the Minister of Trade). I quickly said hello to them, however when I tried to talk to them they were slightly reluctant to engage me in conversation: perhaps they were exhausted with the jubilant crowd. A few moments later, we were invited in the room by one of Barrow's aides to meet with the President-elect. We shook hands with him and sat opposite him. My friend KK introduced me. We had a quick chat about the election campaign, as well as the time Barrow stayed in Forest Gate in London. During our brief conversation, I immediately sensed that he is a very good listener and a humble and gentle man. Before we left I gave him a signed copy of my own book Marriage and Society, and The Prince by Niccolo Machiavelli. He was very impressed with my gift and thanked me for it. As usual, we took some pictures with him, and then proceeded to see his wife, first lady Madam Fatoumata Bah, in the next room. She was very excited to see us. In her room she was surrounded by her family female friends and well-wishers; again I had a brief conversation with her and I gave her a little advice and took pictures with her. Before we left, we had an opportunity to meet with a UDP member called Oudday who was there to assist President Elect Barrow in welcoming well-wishers; I exchanged a few words with her then we finally left.

My second meeting with President Barrow was Tuesday 13th December 2016, during the early days of the impasse. I went to see him with a group of my family and friends; we met him at his new official residence in Brufut Taff presidential villas at around 10 a.m. It was a very constructive meeting. There were many party supporters, people from the media, and members of a private security service guarding the place. Mr Mai Ahmed Fatty from the coalition was also present. We spent nearly two hours in Barrow's residence. While we were there, I gave a speech to the gathering and I assured him of my support and the support of Gambia public. I also encouraged him to politically engage Gambians at all levels. And I asked him to ensure that he strive to unify Gambians. My two friends Alh Batura Jabbi and Ba-Alimameh Jaiteh gave a very impressive speech also. Alh Batura assured him of the support of the Ja-Hankah community in the Gambia. In relation to the political impasse, he prayed for unity among Gambians, as well as assuring President Barrow of our continued loyalty to him and our relentless efforts in offering prayers to him and the nation. President Barrow really appreciated our visit. In his response President Barrow urged us to be good citizens as well as to continue our contribution to socio-economic development in the Gambian and he ensured us that his door was always open to every Gambian who wants participate in national development. After his speech, we left around midday.

I was really touched by Barrow's speech and it has inspired me to re-double my efforts and participate more in national development. It's why I wrote some recommendations to his government through the think-tank which he created in the New Year called the Agency for Socio-Economic Development (ASSED).

Here is what I recommended:

"It is a great honour for me to write you the short recommendation in the following areas: Economy, National Assembly, Agriculture, Constitution and Security Forces. Firstly, I would like to congratulate His Excellency President of the third Republic of the Gambia Mr. Adama Barrow for the trust which Gambians bestowed on him by overwhelmingly electing him on 2nd December 2016 to the highest office in our dear motherland.

Additionally, I commend him for demonstrating in his inauguration speech that he is the President for all Gambians regardless of their tribal or political affiliations; one Gambia, one people. Our expectation of the Coalition Government is huge. Furthermore, by commissioning this "Think Tank", a kind of which has never existed in the history of our country, demonstrates great wisdom from President Barrow. It gives equal opportunity to every Gambian that nation building is our shared responsibility. Hopefully this Agency would serve as a platform for Gambians at all levels to share ideas, common interests and visions for economic development initiatives. We cannot all be politicians or participate in the political process. But providing a channel of communication between politicians and the masses would enable citizens to transmit their opinions to authorities, which will surely cement the relationship between both sides. I hope this agency will be a permanent institution to serve that purpose.

My recommendation for economic development in The Gambia:

There are many economy resources in the Gambia including human resources. However, with the lack of employment and job opportunities in the country many of these human resources especially among the youths are fruitless due to migrating to the west.

1: The Coalition Government should introduce" volunteering semester tax" of at least $300 per annum to encourage every Gambian who is currently living in Europe and America to pay this as their contribution to the national development fund.

2: The Coalition must ensure there is sustainable economic plan which will encourage Gambian intellectuals, experts, and engineers to return and invest their knowledge and experience for nation building.

My recommendation for national assembly reform:

1: The Coalition Government should ensure that, the Presidential decree which allows him to nominate members to the national assembly is increased from five nominated members to twenty nominated members. This nomination should include members of the Gambian supreme Islamic council, Christian council, district chiefs, members from business community, major land owners, and from spiritual institutions like Marabouts.

My recommendation for constitution reforms:

1: The new Constitution of the Republic of the Gambia should include a fixed two five year term limit for Presidency. It must abolish the requirement for a school certificate for any citizens who might want to run for the highest office in the land, whether it's Presidential or national assembly elections as well as Gambians who hold dual nationality. To build the nation should not only be confined to those with certificates of education but it should extend to anyone with genuine political ideas with social and economic skills and have a desire for national development. There are many successful business men and women in the Gambia who have never been to school, however they managed to build successful business empires for their families and communities.

Agriculture reform:

1: The Coalition Government should ensure there are economy plans for food security in the republic of the Gambia which will enable sustainable economy development. To achieve these goals, agriculture will play a crucial role. Thus land reforms laws are urgently needed so that all farming lands cease to be privately owned, rather they should belong to the Government. This would enable the Government to invite investors from within the country and overseas. It must be individuals who are equipped with a variety of farming experience in the area of agriculture. Those new regulations will enable the Government to contract the land by lease to those individuals and companies for a particular period of time including a minimum amount of product they should produce. If they fail to deliver to the Government expectations, they can cease the lease and give the contract to someone else.

Constitutional reform:

1: the new Government must ensure that the Republic of the Gambia Constitution is redrafted and is in line with the 1997 Constitution. All UN necessary amendments done by the former President Jammeh and his regime should be removed from it and it should be respected by all citizens.

Security reforms:

1: The new Government should exercise all their power and influence to ensure they earn the trust, loyalty, respect and command of all security forces in the country. Additionally, they can consider changing the name of the National Intelligence Agency to a different name, perhaps the Gambia Intelligence Service, as well as to relocate their headquarters to different locations in the capital city of Banjul. Unfortunately in my opinion, I think the current NIA is a symbol of torture, oppression and it is allegedly associated with many abuses of human rights in this country. Finally, the current headquarters of the NIA should become the

Gambia history museum.

In conclusion, Gambia is a secular country, the country is known as a republic of the Gambia, not the Islamic republic of the Gambia. And I think it is essential to our national identity to remain at its former name as well as to consider rejoining with the Commonwealth.

My best wishes to the President of the republic of the Gambia His Excellency Mr Adama Barrow and his entire Coalition Government. May God "Allah" bless you and make it easy for you to succeed in all your endeavours."

My recommendation was published twice, by the Point newspaper and the Standard newspaper. Additionally on 22nd February 2017, I handed over a hard copy to the coalition spokesman Mr Halifa Sallah at Kairaba Beach Hotel.

Let's familiarise ourselves with the 2016 Coalition members

Gambia has had many coalitions in the past, however, the 2016 coalition is very unique because they all have one goal and one political enemy whom they are determined to get rid of at any cost. But the future generations might ask who these people are, and why they are in coalition.

Firstly, Hajaratu Fatoumatta Jallow Tambajang was instrumental in persuading the Gambian opposition to unite under one umbrella and remove Jammeh at the ballot box. She is credited with this unique achievement. She was later rewarded with the position of Vice President and Minister of Women's Affairs.

The first member of the coalition is His Excellency President Adama Barrow. He is a long time UDP supporter as well as a member of the party. According to party sources, he once participated in the national assembly election but failed to win a seat from the APRC; He studied in UK and then returned to Gambia to start his real estate business. Before becoming UDP leader in 2016, he was the party treasurer. Adama once claimed that "he is not a politician however it's the will of God for him to become a president". Such rhetoric is common among African politicians. Adama is lucky, like former British Prime Minister David Cameron, however his demeanour is similar to another former British minister, Gordon Brown; a politician who acts like religious leader. When speaks he sounds like a priest or Imam in the mosque. My opinion of him is that he needs to adjust himself a little bit and follow the traditional rules of politics; be a bit more aggressive when it's necessary, otherwise he may be pushed to the side-lines.

The second member of the Coalition is the man I always describe as the adopted child of the Gambia constitution, the Hon. Halifa Sallah. He is the current Secretary General and the leader of the socialist party PDOIS, and he is the current adviser to the President. At one time he was a member of the national assembly during the Jammeh era, but later lost the seat to the APRC. In addition he is well known for his advocacy on civic education in the Gambia. Halifa is a well-liked politician and an educated individual with principles and political convictions. However, he is controversial like the current leader of the UK Labour Party Jeremy Corbyn: articulate, serious and would not be shy to challenge anyone when it's necessary. My take on Hon. Halifa is that he has a disadvantage when he speaks to the public of sounding very gentle and respectful, like a lecturer at a university. Thus he is more like a professor than an African politician. At the end, people are usually cruel to their political leaders and hate them; surely Gambians won't want to hate Halifa and be cruel to him because they perceived him as a good teacher, and students don't hate good teachers. His chance to occupy the high office in the land, though, is very slim.

The third member of the coalition is Hon. Hamat NK Bah, the leader of the NRP since the party was first founded back in 1996, and the current Minister of Tourism. Mr Bah used to serve his constituency as a member of national assembly but he later lost the seat to the APRC. The political style of Hon. Hamat Bah is equal to that of Britain's Nigel Farage. He has confidence, smart and dogged when it's necessary. If his political opponents ignore him, he will take all their supporters. If they engage him in debates, he will probably be better on the stage than they will. My take for Hon. Bah is that there is a lot of potential for him in Gambian politics. However, he must be careful not to use controversial rhetoric.

The fourth member of the coalition is Hon. Mai Ahmed Fatty, the leader of the GMC and the current Minister of Police and the Interior. Hon. Fatty is smart and intelligent, a lawyer transformed to a politician. He is well liked by women and young people. Hon. Fatty is very presentable, as well as ambitious to quickly rise to the top. My take on Mr. Fatty is that with luck he is on the journey to become Gambia's Olusegun Obasanjo (the former Nigerian leader). A politician not only confined to Gambia but the sub-region and the whole of Africa. However, when dealing with his political opponents, he must rely more on his intellect rather than his emotions.

The fifth member of the coalition is Hon. Omar Jallow, known as OJ, the leader of the former ruling party, the PPP, and the current Minister of Agriculture, the same position he held during the PPP regime. OJ is a seasoned politician full of luck and confidence with many political convictions. He is loved and admired by mainly youths and middle class businessmen. During the first republic, he served as Serrekunda's Member of Parliament as well as Minister of Agriculture. After the 1994 military coup, OJ was put on trial with other former PPP ministers by the military junta with allegations of corruption and embezzlement of public funds; however he was later released and cleared of all charges. He faced frequent arrest and torture, but OJ refused to be bullied by Jammeh and his henchmen and remains defiant to the end. Most members of the PPP deserted the party to join with other political parties in the country; however OJ remains loyal to the party as well as to Jawara. OJ is among the handful of politicians who leaves a good legacy in Gambian political history. My take on OJ is that his days of retirement from politics are getting closer. Perhaps it's time for him to write a book and share his political experience with future generations. Whenever I have the chance to listen to him, he reminds me the former Mayor of London, Ken Livingstone. They share the same demeanour.

The sixth member of the coalition is Hon. Henry Gomez, the leader of the GPDP and the current Minister of Youth and Sport. Mr. Gomez is very active in Gambian politics, and participated in the previous election held in the country. However he is not a household name to many Gambians. My take on Hon. Gomez is that he must try to reach Gambian electorates and travel to every corner of the country to try and familiarise himself with voters. He is a well-presented individual and there could be potential for him in Gambian politics.

The seventh member of the coalition is Hon. Blongdeen Bojang, the leader of the NCP. Mr Bojang is a respected medical doctor who used to lead his own political party before he joined the NCP. During the first republic, the NCP was the main political party in the Gambia led by the founder and former vice president of Jawara, Hon. Shrif Mustafa Dibba. However from the late 1990s, the majority of NCP supporters deserted the party and joined other political parties. The NCP party is only a small party in the country. My take on Hon. Bojang is for him to keep on trying: miracles are possible for small political parties, especially when there is need for coalition.

The eight member of the coalition is Hon. Isatou Touray. She is an independent candidate and the current Minister of Trade and Employment. Dr. Touray is a feminist who tirelessly advocates for women's rights in the Gambia, as well as campaigning to abolish female genital mutilation. She is very instrumental in the fight against early child marriage and domestic abuse against women in the country. If you underestimate Dr Touray's abilities in politics, she will rise above all the challenges and win at your expense. She is very intelligent, articulate, attentive, and understanding. My take on

Hon. Touray is that she has proved to Gambian women that their role in society is not confined to motherhood and housekeeping, but they can dream big and achieve big. Definitely there is a future for her in Gambian politics. As a feminist, her luck and political fortune with the ability to persuade people is equal to that of the current Liberian president Madam Johnson Sirleaf. The Gambia is yet to see Hon. Touray's political muscle and the mighty fighting powers which she possesses.

Now that you have a flavour of men and women who unseated Jammeh in December 2016, perhaps you can predict the future and determine what next for the coalition? If you believed in divine power like me, from that perspective one can say it's only possible to remove Yahya Jammeh through divine intervention; however, if you believe in logic and rational thinking, from that perspective you would give all the credit to the talent of these men and women in the coalition.

My opinion about the Coalition 2016

There is no doubt in my mind that the members of 2016 Coalition are talented and dedicated politicians. But they have not yet proved themselves to be different from President Yahya Jammeh. It's the culture of politics to say one thing before coming to power and do totally the opposite once you taste power. In most societies, when humans are in a position of authority they are totally become different creatures. As Gambians, we all know that Yahya Jammeh was gentle and kind before coming to power. However with power it was completely different story. As the English say, politics is a brutal game and for an incumbent to lose the election is bitter pill to swallow. I cannot put it better than British politician Ed Balls. He published a book in which he told some of his personal stories. After he lost his seat in 2015 UK general election, he says in the book "The misery and grief for the incumbent to lose the election is equal to attending your own funeral". If any of those men and women in the coalition lose power, like what happened to Yahya Jammeh, would they react differently?

There is common saying in English "a week is long time in politics". If that is true, five years in politics is equal to one hundred years. Let's say after six months honeymoon for the 2016 coalition, they will start to face the reality of governing. Will they stay gentle and continue to pretend to be innocent as they are now? Or perhaps they will start to be harsh, as is usual in Africa. They have only one big advantage which is that they didn't make any pre-election promises to the agitated nation. Peoples didn't vote for them based on what they heard from them or what they stand for. Instead people voted for them because they were yearning for change to replace Yahya Jammeh with whoever was available.

From my personal perspective, since the election campaign began, I heard one massively impressive statement made by Adama Barrow at his Essau meeting, when he said that "Yahya Jammeh must realise this time that the game is different because he is fighting with people of his own age". This statement later became the slogan of the 2016 election. The following is the fact to vindicate my point:

Even though the coalition knew from the start that they were dealing with a dictatorship; they didn't pre-plan anything. In order to seize the moment, the coalition didn't have any plan for their victory; after Barrow was declared the winner there was no victory speech or shadow cabinet to deal with transition. As result, during the impasse, whenever Jammeh dropped a bombshell, the coalition had to reassemble to make the next move.

This was largely blamed on the fact that this is the first time ever the Gambia experienced transition. Let's give that the benefit of the doubt; however, why did it take them nearly two months to form a simple cabinet? It takes no more than 18 people to run the government of a population less than two million. Were they looking for a rocket-scientist to fix the damaged country?

Equally the coalition had not yet published the memorandum of understanding which stated their agreement terms and conditions, so they can always twist the story to suit their agenda. Now the one million dollar question is: will the coalition stay together for the next three years as they publicly stated; or will they complete the full five year mandate as stated by the Gambian constitution? Will the coalition remain as one unified group to fight the next general election or will they break in to pieces and easily hand over the nation to an APRC and GDC coalition?

Success in African politics, especially in the Gambia, does not required hugely talented politicians who are highly achieving academics. The tools you need the most to succeed in Gambian politics are good luck and social connections. You must engage the people and try to have as many tribal loyalties as you can. Additionally try your best to get good luck from wherever possible, even if it means using the services of spiritual institutions like Marabout and fortune tellers. It's essential to bear that in mind. Whoever wants to occupy public office in the Gambia, this is the secret behind the success.

No one should fool themselves in believing what gave success to Adama Barrow will work for them. Adama was an exceptionally lucky man. He was in the right place at the right time.

In addition to that; I will lend you my astrology skills. His first name starts with the letter A and his last name starts with the letter B. A and B in sequence is a very lucky combination. Also, according his biography Adama was born as one of twins; again in our culture, twins are perceived to be lucky. Third: according to the same biography he was born on Friday. Friday is a holy day for Muslims which mean more luck is added to Adama's basket. Fourthly: his official date of birth is 15/02/1965: if you notice the day starts with the number 1and the year is also starts with 1. Astrologically, these are supposed to be lucky numbers.

I have three major pieces of advice for the coalition government:

1: They must remain together for at least one more general election, because it's almost impossible to achieve any meaningful development in the country in a period of only two years. By then they will start to position themselves to replace President Barrow at next general election.

2: The initial three years agreement in not enough to undertake the urgent political and economic reforms the country needs. They should continue to serve the full five year mandate as stated by constitution.

3: The President must respect the coalition agreement to step out from the office at the end of coalition term whether its three years or five year.

The challenge which could face the coalition government

It's normal for successful governments to face economic as well as social challenges.

Many economic experts in the Gambia predict that the new Gambian government will face huge economic difficulty because the previous regime mismanaged and embezzled the country's resources. Such claims are not new to me and do not make me lose my sleep. If you recall, back in 1964, the UK Conservative Chancellor of the Exchequer Hon. Reginald Maudling told his Labour successor Hon. James Callaghan "Good luck, old cock, sorry to leave it in such a mess".

In 2010 the former Labour Chief Secretary to the Treasury, the Hon. Liam Byrne said to his successor David Laws "Dear Chief Secretary, I'm afraid there is no money." It's common practice to hear politicians use rhetoric like this and blame their predecessors for economic failure. In some cases internal conflict would trigger ministers or insiders to blame their own administrations, for political revenge. As result the so-called financial crime would be only one aspect of those challenges.

When I heard the coalition ministers accuse Jammeh for leaving the Gambia in a total economic mess to the tune of

D48billion (US1billion dollars), I didn't lose any sleep over that. I can still recall back in 1994, Jammeh accused Jawara of the same thing. The former president Abdoulaye Wada in the neighbouring country Senegal experienced a similar accusation from the current leader, President Macky Sall. However, what is really concerning me are the three main serious challenges the coalition might face.

The first challenge is how will they command the respect and earn the trust and loyalty of the Gambian security forces at large in the presence of Ecowas troops, led by Senegal. Given the total isolation of Gambian security forces and their responsibility to Ecomig forces in maintaining peace and order in the country, providing security for the head of state and his government might compromise the trust between the army and the government of the Gambia, like what happened in the 1990s which resulted in a military takeover.

The second challenge is that die-hard supporters of the former regime within the country and outside the country, especially among the security forces, as well as party militants, could create some sort of internal or external sabotage. This could be security related, economic matters, a breakdown in public order, or using social media to compromise the peace and security in the country.

The third challenge is terrorism. Our sub-region is presently a hot spot for terrorists. These enemies of civilisation have no boundaries, they strike any place at any time. And they usually aim at soft security areas in countries where citizens are vulnerable to attack, especially destinations which are very attractive to westerners. Gambia could be at a high risk of such a strike. In the past few years we have seen similar things occur in other countries in our sub-region, especially after a change of government. Such threats remain very real and serious to Gambia.

Note: according one Gambian newspaper report, in late February 2017, Senegal's authorities detained two terrorist suspects who were planning to travel to Gambia. According to that report, one of the suspects was a Malian citizen and the other one was from Mauritania. This is a clear indication that a serious threat from terrorism remains real to the Gambia. Senegal is doing whatever they can prevent Gambia from danger. The foreign policy of the new government in the Gambia is to establish a good working relationship with Senegal. The relationship between the former regime and Senegal was at an all-time low. There was frequent border closure between the two countries, which affected the movement of goods between countries and as a result lost revenue for both countries. Consequently Senegal's government is interested to see the regime change in the Gambia. I think from now on Senegal's government will do whatever they can possibly do will try and control Gambia as well as influence all our political processes. However, Senegal's community were very generous and kind in receiving at least 75,000 Gambian refugees who fled there during the 2016 impasse.

The possibility that Senegal will politically control the Gambia slightly worries many Gambians, including me. The increased presence of Senegal's forces in the country has further exacerbated that, especially when the Gambian government increased the Ecomig mandate to remain in the country for a further three months. I am sure they will use all political means and military tactics to extend that mandate even further.

We have seen similar political control occurring around the world. Big countries always desire to control and influence the politics of their next door neighbours; the example includes United Kingdom's influence in Ireland; France politically controlling Switzerland and socially greatly influencing Belgium; Saudi Arabia politically controlling Kuwait and economically influencing Bahrain. The worst offenders are Russia with their aggression to their small neighbouring countries and the United States has policies on Cuba. There is no ethical foreign policy but the economic as well as the social motive is always there.

One major fact I recently discover in conversation related to politics and religion is; nowadays when you talk about politics and religion, the more you use diplomatic language, the less points you score; however the more you sound like Donald Trump, Nigel Farage, and Jeremy Corbyn, the more points you score.

For Gambia to attain economic super power status in Africa, it's time for the country to stop relying on foreign aid and start the culture of self-reliance. There are many opportunities for the coalition government to look forward to, including Gambian intellectuals willing to invest their experience in the new Gambia. The international communities are more than happy to work with the new administration. The European Union has already made some of their development fund available to the Gambian government and they promise that more help is coming. Gambia's development partners like the US promise to give aid in the way of technical support to the Gambia. In the next few years the country will dramatically improve socially and economically. However, as I stated earlier the government should not entirely base the economic policy on foreign aid. They should explore the country's natural resources as well as other economic methods.

The fight against corruption

Corruption and mismanagement of public funds is a major concern for developing countries. Let's put this on the table: politics is part of corruption and corruption is part of politics. Whatever I might say in relation to corruption is a waste of time unless we collectively tackle the main cause of corruption. In some societies, corruption is due to tribalism, in some bad governance, in some foreign intervention, in some lack of transparency, in some lack of accountability and in some all the above.

Developed countries usually use aggression to invade other countries and rob their resources by pretending they are fighting to restore democracy in those countries. Democracy is just used as a pretext, so that the public won't notice the corruption. That is how most developed countries gain their economic wealth and resources. However, it's a different story in developing countries.

Most developing countries do not have the military capability to invade and rob other countries of their resources with a pretext of imposing their values on them. As result they only have access to internal revenue which the government can loot and quickly run to hide it in the banking system of developed countries. This is what I called external and internal corruption.

Another scenario is that the EU has just recently given a grant of 75 million euros to Gambia's new administration. How come the new government, which is yet to prove to the world whether they are capable of governing or not, gets such a large amount of cash? For what reason, other than it's a bribe to wins future mine contracts as well as politically control the country? That is corruption, but it's done legally and smartly. US President Barack Obama was given the Nobel peace prize a few months after coming to power in order to stop him from using US aggression against other countries. That was corruption; but it was legally as well as smartly done.

Corruption entirely depends on how you define it. To me it's a theory but it's practically impossible to stop it from happening; it's part of human DNA.

Some attitudes are classed as corruption in some countries; however, in others it's perfectly normal, indeed customary. For example in the Gambia, providing a financial gift to a public official is not widely considered as corruption, because giving any kind of gift is part of our culture. Begging is very common in our society and there is no taboo attached to it. Thus often you see police officers in the traffic begging cash from motorists. Such behaviour by public officials is not illegal in our society either. However, this behaviour is illegal in the west because it is considered bribery and corruption.

What is largely perceived as corruption in the Gambia is this: when a citizen needs a public service from an official and the citizen is denied access to that service unless they bribe the official beforehand; this is corruption. Another aspect of corruption is embezzlement of public funds by officials: that is diversion of public funds to the private bank accounts of individuals or officials, who use the funds to line their own pockets.

It has always been common in Africa to donate special gifts to leaders; cash, gold, diamonds, animals, land, or wives, for example. The 13th century Arab traveller and historian, Ibn Batutta stated in his book *Travels of Ibn Batutta* what he saw when he visited the Manding Empire in what is now Mali: "The Negro respect their leaders and they worship them if they wear clothes better than their leader.. in order to show humility before their leader they would throw sand on themselves just to impress him.. they would sit on the floor before him". And he continues "I never saw any human before them who respect their kings and queens more than dark Negro, they give all kind of gifts to kings and queens including humans."

Note: donating expensive gifts to leaders and loved ones does not only happen in Africa. I recalled when President Obama visited Saudi Arabia King Abdullah, he gave a gold necklace as a gift. To show such gratitude to dignitaries by way of respect is common in the Middle East, South Asia, and Africa; it is not classed as corruption. It's still very common practise in the Gambia to donate sheep, chickens, goats and milk to our guests, including family members who return from the Diaspora.

The future of the APRC in Gambian politics

Apart from the NAMs of the APRC aiding Jammeh by declaring a public state of emergency in the Gambia during the impasse, and extending Jammeh's mandate to stay in office, in my opinion, the APRC has not committed any major crimes in the country. Jammeh effectively relied only on his mighty executive power to run the country with very little involvement of the APRC. He used them like he used others. The Gambian public will not hesitate to forgive the APRC. In order to maintain the party support in the country, they must re-group and start some soul-searching which will dictate the future and the direction of the party. In order to prevent disarray in the party they should start to improve the executive committee and replace the old faces with new ones as well as promoting women to more prominent positions in the party.

The current APRC women mobilizer Ms Isatou Jarju could still play an important role in the party, maybe as a potential future leader. That will attract young voters as well as women voters. The members must strive to restore trust in the party executive as well as build the public's confidence in the party immediately. The party loyalists and supporters should change their attitude from the past which could attract more Gambians regardless of their regional and tribal affiliation. The new party rhetoric should be different from the past and it should be more inclusive. The new party manifestoes must include effective economic policies and promote good governance. These should target Gambians at all level.

The Hon. Seedy Njie might still be a useful asset to them. With reform, the APRC under a new leader could do better in the next election than most people anticipate; especially if they have an opportunity to form a coalition with other political parties. They must learn from that which destroyed other political parties, i.e. "All power revolves around the party leader". In that case, when the leader goes, the party loyalists and supporters would desert the party and join with other parties, and often the new ruling party, as we witnessed with the PPP, NCP and GPP.

Did you know that currently the APRC is the main opposition party in the country as well as the most popular? In the 2016 election, the APRC received the highest proportion of votes cast of any single party nationwide. The GDC is the second main opposition party in the Gambia. As we know, the coalition is combined of eight individual political parties, united as one.

167

Here are the votes cast in the last election once more: the APRC received 208487; the GDC received 89768 and the coalition received 227708. If you divide 227708 equally among eight coalition parties, each would receive 28463.5. This analysis might sound crazy to you but we don't know for sure how much a major party like the UDP will poll if they are not in coalition. Would it be hundreds of thousands of votes, several thousand, or just mere hundreds? No matter: it's all guess work. For now let's just go with my analysis.

Based on it, the APRC and GDC are the most popular parties in the Gambia.

Consequently if the coalition of 2016 decides to divorce the marriage and contest the election individually; their chance to lose the election is far greater than winning. If they want stay in power; I suggest to them to stay firmly united until at least after another general election. If the UDP desired to contest the election alone, the risk of losing the election will be even higher, especially if Adama Barrow decides to step aside for a new UDP leader. There is speculation in town that lawyer Darboe will eventually replace Barrow at the end of his term to contest on the UDP ticket.

I am afraid this might throw the UDP into disarray, because under Darboe's UDP leadership in the past, the UDP party failed to persuade other political parties to form a formidable coalition against Jammeh. Returning to the past would surely not be attractive to voters. In my opinion, in order to set a good example for future generations, the prospect of Darboe returning to the leadership should be put aside forever.

What would have happened if Jammeh had won the 2016 election?

I doubt if the demeanour of Jammeh's government policies would have changed at all. However, he might have declared a one political party system in the Gambia. I would not have been surprised if he declared sharia law in the country, and tried to attempt to invade the United Kingdom after Brexit to recover the wealth he always accused them to have looted from the Gambia hundreds of years ago.

Note: the majority of leaders who introduce Sharia law in their country do not do it for the sake of Allah. Usually it's done as a control mechanism. It's not because they love Allah, as they usually claim. Neither is it done for the purpose of giving equal justice for all. With Sharia law, the leaders do not have to take the burden of blame for any crimes committed by them. Sharia law means their leadership is commanded by Allah. Humans would not be able to properly hold them to account. Thus, all shortcomings will be blamed on Allah's will.

If you recall, back in 1995, after mad cow disease in the UK, President Jammeh credited himself for that tragic incident. According to him it was a punishment from God against the British government, who imposed restrictions on their citizens travelling to the Gambia on the grounds that Gambia was not safe after the military coup. As result the revenue from the Gambian tourism industry was badly affected.

In revenge I would not be surprised if Jammeh claims to have contacts from extra-terrestrials to invade the United Kingdom. Do you remember when he withdrew Gambia from the Commonwealth; he published the book "A million reasons why Gambia is leaving the Commonwealth"? I still can't get my hands on a copy of that book. But I think I know who is the brains behind it as well as the brains behind Vision 2016, but I am not ready to share that with readers yet.

My biggest regret is this; why did I not try to meet Jammeh during his 22 year reign? How can I betray myself and not meet the man who was behind the most controversial period in the history of the Gambia; I will leave three questions for readers to answer for me:

Was it a missed opportunity from my side not to try to meet Jammeh personally?

Was it pure bad luck?

Was it pure good luck, because if I met him he might have

169

cast his spells on me to become one of his disciples?

President Jammeh is different from many dictators. He had many good attributes including making sure Gambians, wherever they are, would always keep talking about him. He introduced free education for Gambian children, and he provoked the debate for Africa to rise in the world. His dream of the Vision 2020, for Gambia to attain economic super-power status in Africa.. well, perhaps that may come to pass in his absence. And I think it's essential for the coalition government to maintain free education for children, and the annual Quran recitation competition which Jammeh created to encourage Muslim children to learn and love the holy Quran.

I don't want to have to repeat what happened on 9th December 2016, when I made my prediction of Jammeh's rejection of the election results and his refusal to accept to step down. However, I don't need to be a political genius to predict the coming of a Gambian leader similar to Yahya Jammeh in our lifetime. That will be largely due to what I said earlier: the underlying issues which are prevalent in society.

If I predict that Mamma Kandeh is the potential Gambian leader-in-waiting, would that also be a statement of political genius? We'll wait and see.

As we look forward to the national assembly election in the Gambia, which is scheduled to take place on 6th April 2017, let's hope and pray that it will take place peacefully like the 2016 presidential election. We cannot be complacent; election violence occurred in other African countries like Kenya 2007, Nigeria 2003, Gabon 2016 and Sierra Leone 2007. Let's collectively preach for peace and unity in the Gambia. We cannot accept politicians who divide us for their own political advantage.

I am Yaya Sillah, a Mandinka. My wife is Fulla, my neighbour is Wolof, my father's best friend is Sarahul, my daughter's teacher is Ago, my best student is Jola, and my uncle's wife is Manjack. There is no room for tribalism in the Gambia: it's only one Gambia, one people.

In conclusion, here is my message to Gambia's political class; I always believed in one thing, if the media made any politician famous eventually the media would destroy them. But if you are made by your own talent, then the media will struggle to destroy you. On 2nd December 2016, I saw the euphoria of the election wins and on 26th January 2017, I saw more euphoria when President Barrow returned from Dakar to assume office. On 18th February 2017, I witnessed the mighty euphoria at the Independent Stadium Bakau when Gambia celebrated the 52 independence as well as President Barrow's inauguration.

We must give all our relentless support to President Barrow and his government to take our country from economic as well as social mess. There is no better time than now. I think so far we are heading in the right direction with the right people in the right positions. To build the Gambia to attain economic super-power status in Africa will take collective responsibility and collective participation in national development. We must sacrifice everything today to achieve the best for our future generations. However, it's important to bear in mind that there will be people who wish ill will on the country, some in the country and some in Diaspora. Some participated in the struggle in hoping to get the reward of a job - they will be disappointed if they don't get one. Some participated in the struggle because they want Gambia to economically prosper: those are the people I call patriotic.

However, we must thank all Gambian citizens, both at home and in the Diaspora, for their tireless campaign to restore democracy and good governance in the Gambia.

I would like to extend a special dedication of thanks to all Gambians, especially those on social media. Pa Nderry Mbai, Freedom Newspaper, Fatou Camara, Fatu network Bamba Mass, Kibaaro Radio Suntou Touray, Kairo News and Essa Bokarr Sey, Hello Gambia and all their friends in the media.

The Gambian national anthem

For The Gambia, our homeland,

We strive and work and pray,

That all may live in unity,

Freedom and peace each day.

Let justice guide our actions

Towards the common good,

And join our diverse peoples

To prove man's brotherhood.

We pledge our firm allegiance,

Our promise we renew;

Keep us, great God of nations,

To The Gambia ever true."

ABOUT THE AUTHOR

My name is Alahaji' Yaya Sillah, also known as Yaya–Patchari. I am 41 years old; I was born in Jarra Sutukung Sillah Kunda in the LRR region. I am married with children. I consider my family background to be religious Muslim conservative. Initially my family belonged to the Maliki School of Islamic jurisprudence, but personally I subscribed to the Ash'ari theological school, and my spiritual mentor is Imam Ghazali. However, due to the lengthy time I spent in Western society, my views are more liberal and moderate. Professionally, I follow my Ja-hanka family Marabout tradition, which is essential for guiding people in religious matters and spiritual counselling. I obtained my early Islamic education from my grandfather Alahaji Kebba Sillah Kebba's local Majilis at Jarra Sutukung Sillah Kunda. Later on I furthered my education at Imam Baaba Camara's local Darra at Serrekunda Ebo Town.

Briefly in the late 1990s, I enrolled to study Basic English in night classes in Ebo Town and New Jeshwang, but I am largely self-educated in the language. In 2013, I undertook short courses on Creative Writing in Western Springs College in Auckland, New Zealand, and also as Al-Fridouse Islamic College in Sydney, Australia.

My area of expertise is sociology and spiritual counselling. My first book, published in 2014, was "Marriage and Society", centred mainly on the essence of marriage and the importance of education. Later on the same year, I established my own charity, the Back to School Foundation, the aim of which is to promote education and research in Africa.

Among my hobbies are praying, reading, writing, research, and travelling.

Politics is an area of great interest. This book is based on my own personal experience of Gambia and international politics. It will be very useful for politicians, schools and students.

173

www.ingramcontent.com/pod-product-compliance
Lightning Source LLC
Chambersburg PA
CBHW020245290326
41930CB00038B/379